From Your Freezer to You
Recipes for Every Season

Copyright © 2014 by Nourish & Love, LLC. All rights reserved. No part of this publication may be reproduced or transmitted in any form or by any means, electronic or mechanical, including photocopying, recording or by any information storage and retrieval system, without permission in writing from the Publisher.

This book is not intended as a substitute for the medical advice of physicians. The reader should regularly consult a physician in matters relating to his/her health and particularly with respect to any symptoms that may require diagnosis or medical attention. The author and publisher of this cookbook are not responsible in any manner whatsoever for any adverse effects arising directly or indirectly as a result of information provided in this book.

Inquiries or requests to the Publisher for permission should be sent addressed to:

Stephanie Brandt Cornais
info@mamaandbabylove.com

Produced by Nourish & Love, LLC.
Recipes © Stephanie Brandt Cornais
Photographs © Stephanie Brandt Cornais, Lisa Waszkiewicz
Cover Photo Peter Cornais, edited by Robin Adams Photography

Edited by Leslee Boldman, Managing Editor, Mama and Baby Love and Scott Sweeney
Designed by Aimee Eckhardt, Creatrix Design

To Penelope and Peter, the loves of my life.
You are the motivation for everything I do in life.

contents

INTRODUCTION 1

My Story 1
Real Food is an Investment 5
Eating in Season 6
Take Baby Steps 7
Where To Shop? 7
Grain-Free/Gluten-Free Guarantee 8
Chemical Concerns 9
Natural Sweeteners 10
Flour For Thickening 11
Presoaking 11
Homemade Stock/Broth 12
Mind Your Liquids 12
Slow-Cooked Means Healthy 13

ASSEMBLY 14

Method #1: Freezer to Slow Cooker .. 14
Cooking Time 15
Method #2: Fresh Dutch Oven
Stove Top 16
What Kind of Slow Cooker To Use? 16
Method #3: Fresh Dutch Oven
to Oven 17
Method #4: Brown Meat to
Slow Cooker Food Safety 17
Servings 18
Metric Conversions 19
Cuts of Meat 19
Cooking Fats 20
Kid-Friendly Recipes 21
Wholesome and Simple 21
Create Your Own Slow Cooker
Freezer Recipes! 21

RECIPES 22

FREEZER BAG LABELS 60

recipes

LAMB 22
   Lamb and Beet Stew 22
   Lamb and Fig Stew 22
   Lamb Curry 23
   Moroccan Lamb Stew 23
   Neapolitan Lamb Stew 24

BEEF 25
   Beef Curry 25
   Peppered Beef Stew 25
   Peach Pot Roast 26
   Leek Beef Stew 26
   French Dip Beef Stew 27
   Orange Beef Stew 27
   Saint Patrick's Day Stew 28
   Beef Stroganoff 30
   Sweet & Hot Flank Steak 30
   Pomegranate Beef Stew 31
   Pumpkin Chili 31
   Italian Beef Stew 32
   Nut Stew 32
   Stephanie's Goulash 33
   Spicy Beef Taco Filling 33
   Argentine Beef Stew 34
   Beef Veggie Soup 35
   Ginger Beef 35
   Flank Steak Fajitas 36
   Dijon Beef Roast 37
   Sweet and Sour Brisket 37
   Burgundy Beef 37

CHICKEN 38
   Citrus Chicken 38
   Lemon Chicken 39
   Chicken and Rhubarb 39
   Strawberry Chicken Stew 40
   Chicken Marsala 41
   Mango Salsa Chicken 41
   Chicken Pesto 42
   Honey Apple Chicken 44
   Thai Chicken Curry 44
   Healing Chicken Soup 45
   Chicken and Cherries 45
   Cranberry Chicken 46
   Chicken Curry 47
   Chicken Chili 47
   Asian Ginger Chicken 48
   Polynesian Chicken 49
   Cilantro Lime Chicken 49
   Pineapple Teriyaki Chicken 50
   Apricot Chicken 51
   Tarragon Chicken 51
   Jerk Chicken 52
   Shredded Chicken 52

PORK 53
   Pork and Grapes 53
   Apple Pie Pork Chops 53
   Blueberry Balsamic Ribs 54
   Sausage and Kale Soup 55
   Plum Sauce Pork Chops 55
   Mango Pork 56
   Sausage and Tomato Ragu 56
   Yummy Shredded Pork 57
   Honey Mustard Pork Roast 58
   Pork and Prunes Stew 59
   Harvest Pork Roast 59

My Slow Cooker Freezer Recipes Story

I first started using my slow cooker about eight years ago. At the time, it was emotionally all I could handle. I didn't know how to cook and I had no interest in being in the kitchen because it brought up painful memories of my childhood. It reminded me how much I longed to have a loving and caring mother who cooked meals for me. So, instead of really feeling and owning those emotions, I just stayed out of the kitchen and ate what was familiar and comforting—mostly junk food like potato chips, milk and cereal, and some sandwiches. But one day, I got the urge to buy a slow cooker. I figured I could stand being in the kitchen long enough to chop up some vegetables and dump them in the slow cooker and run like hell. And lo and behold, it worked! With minimal effort, I could actually make a home-cooked meal!

But after a while, even chopping and getting myself organized in the morning before running out the door to work became difficult. And even more difficult when my daughter Penelope arrived. When my daughter was about 4 months old, I got into bulk and freezer cooking and would do long days with a friend to make a month's worth of food. After a couple of times of doing that, I figured there had to be a more efficient and healthier way to prepare large amounts of food.

Then I had my ah-ha moment. I decided to try chopping and assembling ingredients for several slow cooker recipes at once. But instead of cooking them and then freezing the cooked meal in portions, I decided to try freezing immediately after assembly and cook it later.

And again, lo and behold, it worked! I could pull out a meal from my freezer, totally frozen, dump it in my slow cooker, and have a tasty meal ready for my family and I by dinnertime. I felt like I had invented electricity! Both my husband and daughter ate it and loved it! I was so excited! There we were, eating a perfectly healthy, grain-free, dairy-free, made from scratch meal that only took me a couple of minutes to prepare.

I shared about it on my blog, MamaAndBabyLove.com, and later it went bananas viral on Pinterest. I couldn't believe that other people were interested in my idea to streamline freezer prep and slow cooking.

It's been over three years since I started cooking this way and almost two years since my first cookbook came out. I have been floored by the massive amounts of rave reviews I have received about how this way of cooking has changed the lives of moms.

> *Then I had my ah-ha moment. ...*
> *And lo and behold, it worked!*
> *I felt like I had invented electricity!*

These are some of my favorite comments:

"I started using your recipes a few months ago when I went back to work after my son was born. **I have saved so much time and energy!** It is so nice to take one day every couple of weeks and freeze meals away and then the day of drop a bag in the crock pot. Instead of worrying about what I'm making when I get home at 5:30, I know that I just need to prep a side and then dinner is already done. Thank you so much!"

"We have now gotten to try all of your recipes at least once and **we are huge fans!** I made them all one day when I was 34 weeks pregnant and then had my daughter at 36 weeks. We (five of us) have been living on them and I still have 4 more bags to go! Looking forward to the new recipes and my next big cooking day!"

"I just ordered your cookbook and I must say, **your recipes have changed my life!!** I have a 6-month-old son and a very busy work schedule, **I love that I can come home and have a wonderful dinner (and lunches for the next day) ready** for my husband and I with so little clean up. I deal with a lot of guilt about not spending as much time with my son as I would like to because of work, but now I'm able to spend so much more QUALITY time with him in the evenings. Thank you for writing this cookbook, but also thank you for giving me more time with my family!"

"Hi Stephanie! I bought your freezer/slow cooker recipe in anticipation of a huge kitchen renovation. I wanted to have lots of meals for my family ready to go into the crockpot, which is basically the only appliance we have for 4 weeks (and a microwave). I prepped a freezer-full of your recipes in the month before the start of the renovation. I'm midway through the renovation and **have made at least 5 of the recipes already – they are great!** So thank you!!!!"

"I just have to tell you, we purchased the *Back to School* ebook and have loved everything in it. My husband is thrilled that they are not only healthy, but seasoned perfectly. **All I did was follow your instructions!** Thanks!"

But every so often, I would get an email or comment from a mom who was distraught because the recipes didn't work for her and didn't turn out flavorful enough. While those comments have been rare, they haunt me and break my heart. I have always been clear that I am not a chef, but simply sharing an idea that works for me and my family. And now I am so passionate about how this way of cooking because it gives me and other moms more time to themselves—time they can spend taking care of themselves and working on their personal growth and healing journeys—which is the real mission of Mama and Baby Love. So, for over a year, I poured myself into testing and tweaking recipes, and had an army of moms re-test my recipes to make sure my explanations were clear so that all moms have the same success I do with these recipes.

This book explains in more depth, and much more clearly, exactly how I have success with this way of cooking. How to get a flavorful, perfect slow cooker meal EVERY TIME. Be sure to read the entire assembly section before starting. Vital information is in there; the recipes just list ingredients. I hope that, as with me and thousands of other moms, these recipes will fill your home with warmth, love, nutrition and, best of all, delicious food. I am excited for you to begin feeding yourself and your family healthy meals with ease.

Thank you so much for buying my first cookbook and now my second, bigger and better one. My family and I have received so many blessings from your support and I thank you from the bottom of my heart for your continued support. I look forward to continuing to serve you and other moms around the world through my work and through the platform of MamaAndBabyLove.com.

Go forth and cook slowly!

Lots of Love and Light,

Stephanie Brandt Cornais

Founder and Creative Director of <u>Mama & Baby Love</u>

What is Real Food?

I started eating organic foods when I was 19 or 20 and I have only gotten more passionate about food as the years have passed. Reading the book *Nourishing Traditions* by Sally Fallon, and numerous other Real Food blogs, has changed my life.

The moment I heard about Real Food, my whole mind/body/soul knew that it was right and was exactly what I had spent over a decade looking for. I finally figured out what healthy meant.

I still consider myself a Real Food newbie. There are still plenty of recipes I can't make; I get mild anxiety when I make yogurt or water kefir and I can't make kombucha to save my life, but at least I know all the basics like how to soak nuts and grains, and how to make homemade stock. And, of course, I live by the 80/20 rule (which means 80% of the time, I eat perfectly healthy and 20% of the time
I eat what I want) and in general I focus on doing the best I can.

In a nutshell, Real Food is food that is, well, real. Most of the time, if it comes in a bag, box, or package, it is not real. There are some exceptions of small companies packaging Real Food items but 90% of packaged food is not real even if it is labeled organic. Real Food is about cooking in a traditional, homemade way that makes food easier to digest so the nutrients in the food are more easily absorbed. It is about eating wild-caught seafood, and meat from animals that have been pastured and treated kindly at small farms. It is about eating full-fat raw milk, yogurt, and butter. It's about eating organic fruits and vegetables, and buying them in season from local farmers whenever possible, or growing your own.

In essence, Real Food goes against the grain politically and does not agree with the USDA Food Pyramid. The good news is that once you are on board with Real Food, you will realize that all those family recipes that you thought were unhealthy are actually healthy if you focus the quality of the ingredients. Take butter, for example. Fake butter like margarine is not good for you, but real butter made from pastured cows' milk is one of the healthiest things you can eat! So, go ahead and cook with butter, plenty of it! Just make sure it's quality butter. Buying raw butter straight from your farmer is best, but there are some good brands like Kerry Gold that can be found at most grocery chains.

In the two years since my first cookbook came out, I have become more grain free. I am still not 100% grain free, but I am 100% gluten-free and about 80% grain free, or Paleo. I still think that Real Food and Weston A. Price Foundation philosophy is the healthiest way to eat, IF you don't have digestion issues or food allergies. But I think for anyone dealing with digestion issues, allergies, autoimmune issues, or health issues in general, getting off grains is necessary to heal.

> The moment I heard about Real Food, my whole mind/body/soul knew that it was right and was exactly what I had spent over a decade looking for. I finally figured out what healthy meant.

Real Food is an Investment

There are a number of things you can do to be more efficient with your spending and save money but, in general, Real Food just costs more, so get used to the idea of having to spend more money on quality food. It's an investment in yourself and your future. It's easier if you reduce other unnecessary expenses and place a higher value on your family's health. You can expect to spend about 20% of your income on food (more for larger families), which is more than double what the average American spends. Think about the health of an average American and decide how you want your health and life to be. Yes, you may spend more money on food, but you will be reducing medical bills in your future. Eating well is preventive healthcare. If your child eats well, her brain actually has a chance to operate well and she is much more likely to do well in school and get that full ride to college (saving you money!).

> **Eating well is preventive healthcare.**
> Yes, you may spend more money on food, but you will be reducing medical bills in your future.

Eating in Season

There are so many benefits to buying food in season from local farmers and the grocery store. My biggest reasons for eating local, in-season foods, is to eat foods at their peak flavor (making it easier to eat healthy and not want to dive into a bag of Doritos), when they are the most abundant, and (typically) are the least expensive (making it easier to actually afford Real Food). Eating local and in-season foods is . . .

Good for you and tastes better, too.

Locally grown food doesn't travel far, so farmers can choose varieties based on flavor, rather than their ability to withstand a long journey.

Good for the economy.

The money you spend on local food stays in the area as it supports the work of local farmers and markets.

Good for the environment.

The average American meal travels nearly 1,500 miles before reaching the plate. When you eat local food, you reduce the consumption of fossil fuels, carbon dioxide emissions, and wasteful packing material.

Good for family farms.

With each local purchase, you ensure more of the money spent goes to a local farmer.

I know you have had a tasteless tomato or strawberry during the off season and you know what I am talking about. Forcing nature is never a good idea. When you pick a veggie or fruit before it is ripe to accommodate shipping logistics, taste gets compromised.

When you buy produce in season, not only are you supporting your local farmer and getting the most nutritious food in your body (in-season vegetables have more vitamins and nutrients!), but it is also healthier for the earth. Buying food that has the least amount of distance to ship reduces our carbon footprint. Global warming is no joke.

Buying produce in season helps me feel connected to the earth and its seasons. I feel grounded and present and connected in this life by noticing the changes in routine that each season brings. By following what is available to eat each season, I feel alive and in the moment.

In-season produce is at the cheapest price you will find all year long, even at the grocery store. If you stock up and freeze/can/ferment/dehydrate produce while it is in season, you will save a ton of money.

And I also just like supporting small farmers, not just because I am supporting the local economy when I do that, but I liken enlightened, non-industrialized farmers to healers. These days, anyone who feels a calling to be a farmer, and who treats their land and animals with love and respect, is doing a huge service to not only me (the consumer), but to the entire world. To me, they are answering God's call to be of service to Him. I think they are spiritual warriors, sacrificing and leading the way to restore balance to the earth and system.

Take Baby Steps

If you are interested in Real Food, take it slow and make changes as you can. It can be too overwhelming to try and change everything all at once. Pick one thing to change, and once you have mastered that new habit, then move to the next new thing. As long as you are moving in the right direction and slowly transforming your life and the way you eat, you are making progress. One foot in front of the other, one small step at a time, always moving forward.

Where To Shop?

As I said before, the best places to shop are directly from farms and farmers' markets. But beyond that, local co-op grocery stores or natural grocery store chains are the next best option. Costco now even carries some organic and healthy items, like Kerry Gold butter. I also like to shop on Amazon; we are Prime members and then we also do the "Subscribe and Save" option. So on Amazon, I am getting things shipped free, and buying in bulk at Costco prices, but with a wider variety of options, as I can't find things like almond flour at Costco.

Buying groups are still useful, too. Look up your local Weston A. Price Foundation Chapter leader, who will be the key person to know in town and will usually email you when they are going to put in a bulk order of almonds, beef, or cod liver oil.

Just FYI, when you do buy online, clicking to Amazon from MamaAndBabyLove.com, is a great way to support me. I get a small commission on whatever you buy (and since I refuse to have ad network ads on my site- because I can't control the products they run), being an amazon affiliate is my only other source of revenue outside of my own products.   Any product I recommend on my site, is something I actually use and love and rave about to my best friends anyway.

Take Baby Steps.
If you are interested in Real Food, take it slow and make changes as you can.

Grain-Free/Gluten-Free Guarantee

All of my recipes are grain-free, gluten-free, and dairy-free. They also do not include any corn or legumes. Though not technically grains, they are extremely hard to digest and should not be eaten in large quantities if you are trying to heal your body in any way.

My recipes are all Paleo, Whole 30, Weston A. Price, GAPS, and Real Food compatible meals. These recipes do use natural sweeteners in some of the recipes, but if you are eating completely sugar free, you could omit the sugar and the recipe would still be great.

Grains are not the devil, especially if they are prepared properly, but there is a huge misconception about how much grain you need in your diet. If you look at the USDA food pyramid, grains make up the majority of the recommend diet. Really that triangle should be turned upside down, with proteins and fats making up the majority of your diet and grains being the smallest portion.

Grains are incredibly hard on the digestive tract, which directly impacts how much nutrition is being absorbed. Worse yet, grains also contain large amounts of phytic acid, which binds minerals. Even with soaking and sprouting, eating too many grains will be a strain on the endocrine system, as your body copes with digesting these tough, carb-filled plant foods.

I am down to eating one small serving of gluten-free grains a day; often times, I will go several days without any grains at all. Because I crave bread and crackers throughout the day with a meal or snack, I tend to make all my regular meals grain- and gluten-free, so the only additional grains I am adding are a slice of grain-free or gluten-free bread or crackers with one meal. Which essentially, really is just as a treat, and I am not filling up on pastas and grains as a whole. This is has been such a long road for me. Ten years ago, 80% of my caloric intake was carbs and grains!

I like to eat the recipes with a salad and, maybe once every two weeks, I will make a side of white rice. My recipes have enough potatoes in them that I usually don't crave any extra grains for the starch content. You can serve these recipes with whatever you want; if you are a regular pasta eater, serve them over pasta. They taste great over rice or, as a grain-free option, spaghetti squash or cauliflower rice—both amazing ways to add in more vegetables and fill out a meal. Spaghetti squash is super easy to make, just cut one in half, scoop out the seeds and bake it on a baking sheet, filled with a bit of water, placed insides down, in the oven at 350 degrees

Grain-Free/Gluten-Free Guarantee

All of my recipes are grain-free, gluten-free, and dairy-free.

for about one hour. Then use a fork to scrape out the flesh. They will scrape out in small little strings that look like spaghetti. Cauliflower rice is crazy easy too. Just chop up one head of cauliflower into small chunks. Then pulse in a food processor for a few seconds until it looks like rice. Put the rice on a baking sheet, drizzle with a little olive oil and salt, and bake in the oven at 350 degrees for about 30 minutes. Or you could sauté it in a pan on the oven, with a little salt and olive oil, for about ten minutes or until soft.

It may be surprising that I recommend white rice instead of brown rice. While white rice is a grain and, therefore quite starchy, it is still better than brown rice if you choose to eat any rice at all. Brown rice is just rice that still has a hull on it, but the hulls of grains are used as protection for the grain to be able to make it through the digestive tract of animals (i.e., it is not meant to be digested well). As we know, being able to digest our food is critical in being able to get nutrients out. Furthermore, the hull of brown rice also contains phytic acid, which binds what little nutrients your digestive tract can get out to begin with. Optimally, you want to choose white rice and then also soak it first to get the most nutrition.

Quick note about bottled, store bought sauces. Be sure to check and buy only gluten-free sauces. Anytime a recipe calls for soy sauce, you can substitute it with tamari sauce or Liquid Braggs Aminos based on your personal dietary needs.

Chemical Concerns

My recipes also call for a jar of food sometimes. I mention jar in the recipe because, at most health food grocery stores, you can find a jar of tomato sauce versus a can of tomato sauce. I would rather you bought things in a glass jar than a can because of the chemicals in the can, because even cans of organic food items still have BPA in the can. The jar/canned amounts are for ease of assembly, but your best bet is to use ingredients in their fresh, whole forms, so I list that amount as well. Just do the best you can (no pun intended!) and buy food in their whole form when you are able, but don't sweat it if you need to use a jar or can.

While we are talking about BPA, a note about plastic bags: sometimes I get people who ask about freezing food in plastic and if that leaches chemicals into the food. As far as I know, as long as you are not heating your food in the plastic, the chemicals are not released. In the beginning, I only used plastic freezer bags and I feel comfortable doing that because chemicals only leach out from those bags when they are hot (either

Chemical Leaching

I would rather you bought things in a glass jar than a can because of the chemicals in the can, because even cans of organic food items still have BPA in the can.

heating the bag with the food inside or putting food in the bag when the food is still hot). So, as long as you are filling up the bags with cold food, and putting them straight into the freezer, no chemicals should leach out.

But I hated the wastefulness of the plastic bags, so about two years ago, I started experimenting with reusable bags. Through my testing, I found that Neat-Os bags work the best and that is now what I use all the time instead of plastic bags. The only catch with Neat-Os is that they are not liquid proof, so you cannot put any liquids in them and they do not seal 100%, so they are not going to lock out air like a plastic zip-lock bag. And that means they don't last in the freezer as long. A Neat-Os bag will last 3 months in a side door or deep freezer, and a plastic freezer bag will last 6 months in a side door freezer and 12 months in a deep freezer.

I also do not recommend using the slow cooker liners that are on the market. I know it is tempting to not have to clean up your slow cooker, but heating plastic at that high of a temperature, even BPA-free ones, is not a good idea, my friends. If you rinse your slow cooker right away, instead of letting the food harden and cake to the sides it is much easier to clean up. If some food does stick a little bit, use a sprinkle of baking soda to help you scrub.

You also want to be cognizant of the slow cooker you buy. Old slow cookers, and even some new ones, can have lead in them. It's best to buy the highest quality slow cooker you can afford and if you ever get a crack in the ceramic insert, throw it out. The lead can be found in the ceramic insert, but is likely to only leach out if there is a crack in the glaze. And while we are on that topic, you can crack a ceramic insert by not having enough food in the slow cooker while cooking. Your slow cooker needs to be ¾ full to work properly. If it has less food in it, the insert gets hotter and, not only does the food cook faster, it can crack your insert.

If ever water is called for in a recipe, I use filtered water. There are so many chemicals in our local tap water that I don't just use filtered water for drinking but for cooking as well. I have a huge water filter that filters out everything, it's a pain to fill it up, but I think it's worth it because there are so many chemicals in the world and I can't control my exposure to all of them, so I try to control and manage what I can.

Natural Sweeteners

I use rapadura sugar, coconut sugar, or date sugar instead of regular white sugar. All of those can be substituted for white sugar in a one-to-one ratio.

Those natural sugars are not stripped of nutrients from processing, and they don't spike your blood sugar as much. So, while still sugar, they are just a little bit better for you. When a recipe calls for 2 tablespoons of sugar, you can pick whatever sugar you want, but try out a natural type if you haven't before.

There are several different natural sweeteners on the market right now. I stay away from Stevia and Agave; Stevia has a funky aftertaste, and Agave is no better than corn syrup as it is chemically processed. In general, I stick with rapadura, coconut, or date sugar; shredded coconut; chopped or pureed dates; honey; and maple syrup.

Flour For Thickening

I use arrowroot flour, also sometimes called arrowroot powder, it is as a healthy, gluten-free thickening agent for sauces and stews. Tapioca will work, as well. Cornstarch or regular flour are more obvious choices, but they are obviously not grain free or gluten free.

In each recipe, I list 2 tablespoons of arrowroot powder to thicken the liquid in the recipe. Refer to the Mind Your Liquid section to see how to get the perfect consistency you desire.

If you are doing the original slow cooker freezer method, you will just sprinkle the flour in the bag along with the other spices and ingredients. If you are doing a Dutch oven method, you will use the flour when you season the meat before browning.

Presoaking

There are several other processes to learn in order to make food the most digestible it can be, including soaking grains (including rice) and beans. This is done to help reduce the amount of phytic acid in the beans. Phytic acid binds to magnesium, iron, zinc, and calcium, preventing you from absorbing these essential nutrients. The process of soaking breaks down the phytic acid and makes these nutrients more bio-available (easier for your body to absorb).

To soak dry beans or rice, simply put your selection in a big bowl or jar with room for expansion, add at least a tablespoon of an acidic medium (such as vinegar, lemon juice, or fresh whey). Then fill with water to completely cover and soak overnight. If soaking almonds or other nuts, soak them in warm salt water—no acidic medium is needed; you will want to dehydrate them for 24 hours at a low temperature (between 115 and 150 degrees) to make them crispy again.

Homemade Stock/Broth

I also mention chicken or beef stock in many of my recipes. Homemade stock is far superior to anything you can buy in the store; it literally is one of the most nourishing foods on the planet. When I first starting cooking in a Real Food way, making stock was one of the first things I set out to do. I figured between switching to raw milk and making homemade stock, those two alone made major leaps in good health for my family and I could slowly learn the remaining traditional cooking methods as I went along. I have a great tutorial on how to make your own chicken stock on my blog, just search for it in the right hand corner of the menu tab at the top.

An easy way to make chicken stock in your slow cooker is to put an entire chicken carcass and bones from a roast chicken you made into your slow cooker and fill it with three cups of filtered water. Add salt and pepper to taste and cook on low for 8 hours. Then when the stock is done cooking, remove the bones and pieces and strain out anything else. When the stock is cooled, divide it into 1- or 2-cup portions and pour into small sandwich freezer bags and lay flat and stack in your freezer. Then take out what you need as you need it.

Mind Your Liquids

In most of these recipes call for about 1 cup of liquid. And, in general, you will need to add less liquid to a slow cooker, because no liquid gets evaporated. And there is also liquid from the freezing process. In the Dutch oven ways, liquid gets cooked down and you will usually need to add more liquid.

Also, these recipes can leave you with liquid from the sauce or stew (if you do not adjust thickening agent and amount of liquid to start with to your personal preference at the beginning), because liquid does not evaporate in a slow cooker as with other methods of cooking. But this is good stuff, don't throw it away! You can freeze it in an ice cube tray and use it later, or put it in your fridge to drink a mug with your lunch. It's great if you can get in the habit of drinking a cup of broth a day. Personally, that is hard to do—just sit and drink broth; I have to really force myself to do it. But that is another reason I love to have stews for dinner . . . I get my cup of broth in much easier!

But if you want to thicken your liquid, after your meal has been cooked, scoop out a cup or two of the liquid and put it in a sauté pan over high heat and reduce it down (that brings bring it to a boil and then let it simmer until there is less liquid). You could also add in more thickening agent and whisk it into a roux. When you are done, you add it back to the slow cooker and give it a good stir. If you want more liquid at the end, just add more at anytime in the cooking process and let it cook another 30 minutes.

If a recipe calls for juice, do what you can to make the juice yourself. Unpasteurized, raw, fresh juice is tastiest and healthiest for you. But of course you can use store-bought juice, too.

Slow-Cooked Means Healthy

These recipes are awesome because they save you so much time, but they are also so healthy. Not just because of the broth, and all the meat and vegetables and healthy spices in them, but in the way they are cooked. Cooking your food slowly means it is easily digestible. Whether you have poor digestion or not, it's good to add soups and stews into your diet and give your digestion a break whenever you can. Especially if you are a new mom! These recipes are perfect new-baby-in-the-family meals to make life easier for mom, but also to help heal and restore mom from childbirth. Ayurvedic wisdom says that a new mom should only eat soups and stews for 40 days after the birth of her baby!

I also did not include calorie information of these recipes. Even though I stopped counting calories years ago, I know a lot of women count calories and it is important to them; I tried to be accommodating in the first cookbook. But as I work with mothers, helping them with weight loss and learning to love themselves just as they are, I find it is more important than ever to stress not counting calories as a way to be healthy. So, I purposely did not include calorie info for these meals because no matter the calories, these recipes are the gold standard as far as health goes. There is nothing else you could be eating for dinner that is healthier than a grass-fed animal protein and fat, organic vegetables, spices, and broth. I urge you to stop counting calories and focus on making good food choices. Eating less sugar and grains and more protein and fat is what will keep you slim.

Ayurvedic wisdom says that a new mom should only eat soups and stews for 40 days after the birth of her baby!

Assembly

In my first cookbook, I only explained one way to do these recipes—the chop, assemble, freeze, and dump in the slow cooker the day of cooking way. This is the way that I came up with that started this whole idea and the way I make these meals 75% of the time. But as my culinary chops have improved these past two years, I have experimented with other ways of cooking these recipes that are still very easy, but are different than the original method.

So in this cookbook, you have four different options to cook these recipes, depending on how much time you have and your families' unique palate.

If you go the other ways of cooking, you can chop your vegetables and keep them in the fridge, in a sealed container, up to a week ahead of cooking.

Method #1:
Freezer to Slow Cooker

Combine all ingredients (except liquid-and by liquid I mean stock/broth, tomato paste, soy sauce which is added on assembly day) into a 1-gallon-sized freezer bag.

On the day of cooking, place contents of bag into your slow cooker and add liquid. Cook on low for an average 8 hours or on high for an average of 4 hours. Add a bit more salt, pepper, and other spices to taste and stir well the last 30 minutes of cooking.

For my traditional slow cooker freezer recipe method, I prefer preparing three recipes at a time because this is the most manageable for me. If you want to do one recipe at a time or 10, go right on ahead and do what works for you. I like prepping three at a time because it only takes a couple of hours, including cleanup. The more veggies you have to chop, the longer it can take. Each meal gives my small family leftovers, and as I don't cook a slow-cooker meal every day (I like to keep it varied and do simple one-dish meals once or twice a week), this is all I need to do to have a month's worth of meals in my freezer.

Before you assemble your meals, chop all your vegetables. Sometimes I chop all the veggies the night before, or the afternoon I buy them, and store them in gallon-sized freezer bags in my fridge. The next day, I reuse the same freezer bags for the meal assembly. As with all things I set out to accomplish, I break the task into smaller, more manageable steps.

Next, line up all your ingredients, grouped by recipe, on the kitchen counter for quicker assembly. If you haven't already put in all the veggies in the gallon freezer bag first, then clean up a bit and get ready for the meat.

I hate handling raw meat. So, if I don't buy large quantities of meat from a local farmer, I will ask the butcher at the grocery store to cut up the meat for me. If you don't mind touching meat, you could chop up the

Chop.

Assemble.

Season.

Freeze.

meat into 1-inch cubes. Or you can do like me and leave it whole, cutting up the meat after it is cooked when it is so tender, it really just falls apart. In fact, most of the time, I just need to give the meal a good stir and the meat breaks up into bite-sized pieces easily.

You add the meat to the freezer bag on top of the veggies. **I add the meat second, so that the spices can go directly on top of the meat, to make sure the meat gets all the spices.** You can put the meat in a separate bag, if you wish. There is no issue with combining raw veggies and raw meat if you are putting them straight into the freezer, then straight into the slow cooker the day you cook. If your pieces of meat are already frozen, just omit the meat completely and only do veggies and spices. Then, on the day of cooking, take out your corresponding cut of frozen meat from the freezer with the corresponding bag of frozen veggies and spices and dump it all in together. If this is what you do, be sure to add more spices to your meat once it's been cooked a bit, since it did not get any spices on it during assembly.

Finally, I close the freezer bags and shake to mix it up a little bit, then I lay it down flat so it freezes like a thin, flat brick. This saves room and makes the freezer nicer to look at. I don't know about you, but I love anything lined up in a nice row or stack. I either handwrite the contents on the bag using a Sharpie pen, or I use the labels provided in the back of this cookbook, which are Avery 8163 compatible.

On the day of cooking, I dump the contents of the bag into the slow cooker. If the contents of the bag are on the smaller side, I can usually put it in the slow cooker and get the lid on without any problems. If it is a bigger meal, I let the bag sit out for a few minutes to let it thaw just enough so I can mash it with a wooden spoon and break it up into two or three big frozen chunks. (Also note that I have an All-Clad 6-quart slow cooker, which is bigger than most.) Sometimes I need to cut open the gallon freezer bag, but most of the time the contents just slide out into the slow cooker, especially after I have the brick sit on the counter for a few minutes-that is all that is needed for it to thaw enough to slide out easily. And sometimes the spices stick to the bag and I need to scrape the sides of the bag to put the last bit of the spices in the slow cooker or I will put a couple of tablespoons of water into the bag and swish it around to un-cling the last of the spices and then I just pour that liquid/spice mixture into the slow cooker.

The morning of the day of cooking is when you add your liquids. You do not add liquids to the bags during assembly, even if you are using plastic freezer bags. If you have room in your plastic freezer bag and you really wanted to, you could if you wanted. However, the way I do it is liquid on the day of cooking. I do this because I make all my stock and freeze them individual one-cup servings. I take out what I need, as I need it.

Cooking Time

All the cooking times that I have listed are approximate. What I have listed is what works for me in my kitchen with my slow cooker and my oven. There are a ton of slow cookers on the market, all different sizes that heat differently, just like ovens. Some run hotter when cooked in the high mode and some run hotter when cooked in the low mode. You really have to get to know your slow cooker and make adjustments as necessary to get these recipes to turn out in your slow cooker. The amount of food in relation to the size of your cooker matters, so if you have too much or too little food in your cooker, it can affect the way your food turns out.

While getting to know your cooker, pay attention when you make a brand new recipe and then make notes for the next time you cook the recipe. Did you overcook it and it needs to be taken out sooner next time? Or was it a little tough and needed another hour? In general, chicken and pork cook faster than beef, but keep an eye on your meals as you get to know your cooker and get used to this style of cooking.

Get to know your cooker, and pay attention when you make a brand new recipe and then make notes for the next time you cook the recipe.

If you are home while your meal is cooking, resist the urge to open the lid and stir it. I used to love to do that, so I felt like I was actually doing something, but it lets so much heat escape when you do that, so just enjoy your time not having to be in the kitchen stirring something.

The last 30 minutes of cooking, you need to check your meal and add more spices to it and give it a good stir. I usually just add more salt and pepper, but I will also add some more spices from the recipe whether it was cumin or thyme. This is a crucial step to ensure flavor. Season it to your taste and your family's preference. Also check liquid levels. If there is not enough liquid, you could add a little water. If there is too much, you could scoop out a cup or two and put it in a hot sauté pan on the stove top to reduce it down (that means bring it to a boil and then turn down the heat and simmer it till about half the liquid or more is gone) and then stir it back into the stew.

Many slow cooker recipes call for browning meat before adding it to the slow cooker. This is to enhance the flavor of the meat. However, in my experience, and the experience of the moms I had testing these recipes, is the recipe tastes the same either way, so why add an extra step? I realize I am not a fancy chef and I grew up eating Doritos for dinner and my taste buds are of the simple kind, but my recipes are eaten and enjoyed by my family and friends when I make my recipes without browning and doing the assembly, freezer to slow cooker, dump and run method. If you follow all the directions carefully, you will get a tasty meal doing it this way. BUT ... if you are a fancy chef and have much more discerning taste buds than me, or want to use these recipes for entertaining, then read on; there are other extra steps you can do to enhance the flavor of these recipes even more.

Method #2:
Fresh Dutch Oven Stove Top

Chop all vegetables. Heat a Dutch oven to medium-high heat and then add the cooking fat/oil. Combine spices and flour and season meat. Brown the meat for an average of about 4 minutes each side. Remove browned meat. Add vegetables in the same Dutch oven with residual fat and cook until soft and fragrant, about 5 minutes. Then add liquids and scrape off all brown parts and pieces on the bottom of the pan and stir well. Add meat back in, cover with lid, and bring to a high, rolling boil for a few minutes (really, just a few minutes or it will burn) and then

What Kind of Slow Cooker To Use?

I use an All Clad 6-quart slow cooker and I also have a 4 quart one. The 6 quart cooker is, is the largest on the market and, honestly, one of the most expensive. However, I have had it almost 8 years and it works fantastic. I think you get what you pay for in slow cookers and it is worth the investment, especially if you are going to use it as much as I do.

Whatever kind you buy, a programmable one is a must if you are going to not be home while cooking. You will to be able to program it and have it automatically switch to warm for you while you are away. Some even have browning options and rice cooking settings, which are awesome too.

And as I mentioned before, not only do old slow cookers not have programmable options, they may contain lead. It's best to just toss out the old one and buy a new one if you are going to really incorporate this way of cooking into your life.

Buy the right size for your family. If you are single, you probably will only need a 3- or 4-quart slow cooker (and, in that case, just reduce my recipes by half). Larger families, or smaller families like mine that love leftovers, would do well with a 5- to 7-quart slow cooker. Whatever size you get, again you need to make sure the slow cooker is at least ¾ full to work properly. If you have a bigger slow cooker but are cooking a smaller portioned meal, put a glass, oven-safe dish in the slow cooker first and then put in your ingredients to help fill it up.

I like having two slow cookers because I often have both going at once, one cooking stock or rice and other making a meal.

turn to low. Simmer on low for about 1.5 to 2 hours. Check it at 1.5 hours to determine if it is done or needs more time.

Method #3:
Fresh Dutch Oven to Oven

Chop all vegetables. Heat a Dutch oven to medium-high heat and then add the cooking fat/oil. Combine spices and flour and season meat. Brown the meat for an average of about 4 minutes each side. Remove browned meat. Add vegetables in the same Dutch oven with residual fat and cook until soft and fragrant, about 5 minutes. Then add liquids and scrape off all brown parts and pieces on the bottom of the pan and stir well. Add meat back in, cover with lid, and put the Dutch oven into your oven set at 325 degrees and cook for about 1.5 to 2 hours. Check it at 1.5 hours to determine if it is done or needs more time.

Method #4:
Brown Meat to Slow Cooker

Chop all vegetables, or pull out bag of pre-chopped veggies from the freezer. Heat a large Dutch oven or fry pan and turn on to medium-high heat. Add cooking fat/oil when hot. Combine spices and flour and use half to season meat and add to hot oil. Brown the meat, about 3 minutes each side. Then transfer meat to your slow cooker. Add rest of spices, liquid, and vegetables to slow cooker and cook on low for 8 hours or on high for 4 hours. Add a bit more salt, pepper, and other spices to taste, if needed, and stir well the last 30 minutes of cooking.

I love that I can come home and have a wonderful dinner (and lunches for the next day) ready for my husband and I with so little clean up.

Food Safety

It goes without saying, but I should cover my butt and go ahead and say it: Start with a clean kitchen and a clean slow cooker. New slow cookers reach a high enough temperature, even on low, while cooking that it kills any bacteria that may have gotten in while preparing your meals. If the power goes out while you are cooking your meal and you have been gone all day, throw it out. It's not worth the risk.

Once you have finished cooking your meal, put leftovers in the fridge within 2 hours. I will usually turn off the slow cooker as I am serving dinner and leave the lid slightly ajar so it can cool down a bit before I put the leftovers in the fridge. It is totally fine to refreeze leftovers if you want too. If we have a lot of leftovers and I know we are going to be eating off it for a couple of days, I will immediately portion out a couple of individual portions for the freezer, so that when we get sick of eating it after three days, I don't waste any of it.

The USDA official recommendation is to not put frozen food into your slow cooker. I have always put my food in completely frozen and they come out great. These recipes will still work fine if you want to thaw them first and put them in your slow cooker. If you do thaw it first, thaw it in your fridge, not the counter or sink. I would recommend putting the bag on a plate or dish in your fridge, in case it leaks as it thaws, it won't mess up your fridge. Or, if you are home and it makes you feel better, you can put in the frozen contents into your slow cooker, but cook it on high for 1 hour and then turn it down to low for the rest of the cook time.

Blanching, Freezing, and Cooking Vegetables

I get lots of questions about whether or not to blanch the vegetables. I do not blanch my veggies before freezing. Onions, green peppers, beets, and carrots—all veggies that I cook with a lot because they hold up well in a slow cooker—do not require blanching. Period. If you want to blanch the other vegetables, go right ahead.

Blanching can help improve the flavor, texture, and color of the vegetable if you are sautéing or baking it, but vegetables will get very soft in the slow cooker regardless. They will get coated in the sauces or stew, obscuring those things blanching might preserve, so I figure there's no point. I also end up eating all my freezer meals within a short time period, so there is no need for blanching to help extend freezer time.

Yes, I freeze potatoes, both white and sweet. The white potatoes do change color, but it's only a marbling. It does not affect the taste of the potato at all. Again, all the veggies become covered in the sauce or stew spices, so who cares? If you do not want to freeze your potatoes, that is fine, too. Just chop and add them the day of cooking. For my recipes that call for potatoes, you can use red, russet, or sweet potatoes unless specified. Any of those options of potato will work fine; just choose what you want for your family's dietary needs and tastes. If you are doing yeast cleanse or sugar detox, and do not eat potatoes at all, just omit them and the recipe will still work.

Pretty much any vegetable you cook in the slow cooker is going to be soft. If you don't like mushy vegetables, don't use your slow cooker! Alternatively, you can freeze them in a separate bag, sauté, stir-fry or bake them separately and mix them in after your meat is cooked or serve as side. You can also try adding them to the slow cooker the last hour or half-hour of cooking and see how you like them that way.

I use a lot of vegetables like root vegetables and hardier vegetables that hold up well in the slow cooker. Tender vegetables—like asparagus, spinach, and peas—do not do well. These kinds of vegetables must be added the last thirty minutes of cooking, that is all they need.

I think the best option is to cook the recipes as-is, and serve a side of fresh salad greens or roasted or sautéed veggies.

Also, when I say 1 cup of chopped onion, I mean to chop it into about 1-inch pieces. Anything that just says to be chopped is meant to be coarsely cut and pretty big. Minced means to chop into tiny pieces. And

Servings

In my first cookbook, my recipes were doubled and filled two bags. But that was just too confusing for folks. These recipes are all large sized meals, but not doubled, with an average of 6 to 8 servings. If you want to double the recipe, you will need to double all ingredients. You may, on occasion, not be able to fit everything into one bag. In that case, just split all the ingredients into two separate bags.

If you have a small family or are single, you can split these recipes into up to four bags to make smaller meals with fewer servings. Or you can make the large meal, but freeze the leftovers in individual portions.

Each recipe will fit into a gallon-sized freezer bag, so if you double the recipe, you will need two bags. Some recipes will leave the bag stuffed to the brim and others will have more room in them, but they will all fit in one, 1-gallon freezer bag. Each bag is one meal, consisting of an average of 6 servings; some are more, and some are less. For my small family, each bag becomes dinner that night and several meals of leftovers.

Get to know your cooker, and pay attention when you make a brand new recipe and then make notes for the next time you cook the recipe.

just FYI, to make grocery shopping easier, 1 cup of chopped onion usually equals about 1 medium onion. One pound of vegetables is usualy about 3 to 4 cups.

Cuts of Meat

My recipes call for 3 pounds of meat because that is a good portion of meat for a 6-quart slow cooker. If you end up using a little more or a little less, that is totally fine. Some people like to reduce the amount of meat to save money and reduce meat consumption.

For the chicken recipes, unless it is specifically noted, you can use breast, thighs, or other bone-in pieces. Bone-in cuts can usually be cooked longer, so if you know you will be out of your house for 8 hours or longer, go with the bone-in option.

For the pork recipes, use some sort of pork loin roast, unless specifically listed as something else like pork chops or ribs. A pork loin roast is a general term and the cut can look differently. Try to find the ones that are wider and fatter; they hold up and fit better than the long, skinny ones.

Chicken and pork are easy to work with, but keep in mind that they dry out more than beef. They can't be cooked quite as long as beef, so be extra vigilant the first time you make a new chicken or pork recipe.

Of my recipes that call for beef, there are lots of different types of beef stew meat to choose from: chuck, bottom round, rump roast, and sirloin. I also use a lot of flank steak. You can use any of these cuts interchangeably for my recipes that call for beef stew meat or flank steak. I always use organic, grass-fed beef. It is so much healthier for you, and has as much omega-3's as salmon.

Metric Conversions

U.S. = Metric

¼ teaspoon = 1.25 milliliters

½ teaspoon = 2.5 milliliters

1 teaspoon = 5 milliliters

1 tablespoon (3 teaspoons) = 15 milliliters

1 fluid ounce (2 tablespoons) = 30 milliliters

¼ cup = 60 milliliters

⅓ cup = 80 milliliters

½ cup = 120 milliliters

1 cup = 240 milliliters

1 pint (2 cups) = 480 milliliters

1 quart (4 cups; 32 ounces) = 960 milliliters

1 gallon (4 quarts) = 3.84 liters

1 ounce (by weight) = 28 grams

1 pound = 448 grams

2.2 pounds = 1 kilogram

Spice it Right

I tend not to go crazy with the spices because my husband has a sensitive stomach. I love spicy foods, so I consider these recipes to be a nice middle ground. But please feel free to increase or decrease the amount of spices in these recipes to your families tastes.

As I am using high-quality ingredients, my taste buds are tuned to the subtle, rich flavors rather than the overly salty, sugary, MSG-laden processed stuff you find in cans and spice mixes. It's just like going without any sugar for a while, and then trying a piece of fruit, or even a glass of milk, and finding it far sweeter than you remember. So, keep that in mind as you go on your health journey; your taste buds will evolve with you as you stop loading up on sugary drinks and processed packaged food.

Also keep in mind that cooking in a slow cooker for long periods of time, in liquid, can reduce the intensity of some spices. Like I mentioned before, the last hour to half hour of cooking is crucial; if you feel like your meal needs a bit more kick, I would recommend adding more of the spices. And as I mentioned earlier, taking out some of the liquid and reducing it in a saucepan is also a way to increase the flavor of the liquid and meal. Scoop out a cup or two and put it in a hot sauté pan on the stove top to reduce it down and then stir it back into the stew.

If your meat is already frozen and you just assembled the vegetables and spices, be sure to spice your meat about thirty minutes in and for sure at the end of cooking, as it didn't get in the spices during the assembly process.

Be sure that your spices are fresh. You will be amazed how quickly they go bad. If you have had cumin in your spice cabinet for years, throw it out! I like to buy my spices in bulk so I can buy a couple tablespoons at a time, so I always have fresh spices, and because it reduces waste. I reuse the same spice bottles over and over again. And because I am OCD and I like having all my spice bottles look identical.

The most flavorful way to use spices is the traditional Ayurvedic way of toasting or sautéing whole spices, cardamom for example, and then after the whole spice is browned a bit and toasted, you grind it up. The toasting brings out so much flavor and keeping the spice whole, until day of cooking, ensures absolute freshness.

When picking a wine to use in these recipes, be sure to pick a wine that you would actually want to drink. Lean towards dry, medium-bodied wines that are not too sweet and not too strong.

A quick note about salt: My recipes all call for salt. Please know that you should salt all these recipes to taste. Don't be shy with the salt. It is one of the requirements in cooking to bring out flavors and have a tasty meal. So, if all else fails, just salt the heck out of your meal!

And don't feel guilty about the amount of salt either! Salt is a very important nutrient for your health. Each cell in your body is regulated in a masterful way based on sodium levels; so, for your body to function properly, you need salt! However, sea salt is the kind of salt you need to use; table salt is not good for you.

Cooking Fats

If you are going to cook these recipes in the Dutch oven stop method, Dutch oven-oven method, or simply brown your meat first before putting it in the slow cooker, you will need some sort of fat or oil to brown your meat and veggies in. Through this cookbook, if you are going to do the browning methods, you will need some sort of fat to brown the meat. You can use whatever you want, and will usually need 1 to 2 tablespoons of it, but if you want to go for healthy fats, try coconut oil, lard, bacon grease, or olive oil.

It is a misconception that fat is bad for you. You actually need fat for your brain, hormones, and body to work properly. And many vitamins and nutrients are fat-soluble and the only way for your body to absorb them is with some sort of fat.

So please stay away from canola and other fake oils and instead liberally cook with healthy animal fats and healthy oils, like coconut and olive oil.

Kid-Friendly Recipes

All of my meals are suitable for kids older than about 10 months to eat. Slow cooker meals are awesome for babies and toddlers because the meat and veggies are so soft and easy for them to chew and digest. We did Baby-Led Weaning with Penelope, meaning she never got pureed food; we just gave her bits and pieces of whatever we were eating. But if you are super-excited about making pureed baby food, once you have introduced meat to your baby, all you have to do is take a cup of the slow cooker meal and toss it into a food processor or use an immersion blender to blend it up into a puree that you can spoon feed your sweet babe.

Wholesome and Simple

Lastly, these recipes are for your weekday family dinners. They are tasty, wholesome, nutritious, and easy to prepare. They are not something amazing that you cook to impress your friends at a dinner party-because they are not the prettiest meals to look at. This is a way to pull a meal straight from your freezer, no thawing, no second thoughts, and dump it into your slow cooker so that you can put a healthy and tasty meal on the table for your family without slaving away in the kitchen for hours on end. These meals are the workhorse of your kitchen, the foundation of your freezer stash.

Slow cooker freezer recipies are perfect meals for busy families. These meals are always in my freezer, so if I have a busy day or week, these meals are there for me. It takes the pressure and stress off of constantly having to plan a meal. If I need to deliver a meal, no problem, I just grab one out of my freezer.

> *These meals are the workhorse of your kitchen, the foundation of your freezer stash.*

Create Your Own Slow Cooker Freezer Recipes!

Creating a new recipe is one of the best parts of being in the kitchen. The sense of pride of making something unique and tasty is fun and empowering. And it is a great creative outlet. I am firm believer that the more use your creative brain, the more creative you become as person.

There is a pretty simple formula to making these recipes and, once you know it, you can turn some of your family favorite recipes and flavors and convert them to this way of cooking.

Basically, you need 3 pounds of meat and about 2 pounds of vegetables and about 1 cup of liquid (whether the liquid is diced tomato in juices, wine, stock, or sauce). To keep the right consistency of a stew, keep the liquid to around 2 cups total.

For spices, think about the flavor combinations of your favorite recipes and try them with slow cooker meats and vegetables. And one of my favorite books is called the Flavor Bible. It tells you what flavors and spices pair well together and it is a wealth of information to springboard your creativity.

Lamb

Lamb and Beet Stew

3 pounds lamb sirloin roast

3 cups beets, peeled and sliced

3 cups potatoes, peeled and cubed

5 teaspoons freshly minced mint (or 1 tablespoon dried)

3 teaspoons freshly minced rosemary (or 1 tablespoon dried)

½ teaspoon lemon zest

5 cloves garlic, minced

1 teaspoon salt

1 teaspoon ground black pepper

2 tablespoons arrowroot flour

Day of cooking:

1 cup beef stock

3 tablespoons lemon juice

Lamb and Fig Stew

3 pounds lamb, diced into small chunks

1 pound figs, cut in half, stem removed

1 cups onion, chopped

1 pound carrots, chopped

2 garlic cloves, minced

1-inch ginger root, peeled and minced

1 teaspoon ground cinnamon

2 tablespoons arrowroot powder

Day of cooking

4 cups chicken stock

slivered almonds *optional garnish

Please refer to the Assembly section for preparation instructions.

Copyright © 2014 Stephanie Brandt Cornais | Mama & Baby Love
Content may not be reproduced in whole or in part without express written consent.

Lamb Curry

- 3 pounds boneless leg of lamb, cut into 1-inch cubes
- 1 pound potatoes, peeled and chopped
- 3 cups okra, chopped
- 4 cups onion, chopped
- 12 tablespoons fresh ginger, peeled and minced
- 12 garlic cloves, minced
- 2 green chilis, cored, de-seeded, and sliced
- 4 teaspoons paprika
- 4 teaspoons ground coriander
- 8 teaspoons cardamom
- 4 bay leaves
- 4 teaspoons cinnamon
- 3 teaspoons turmeric
- 2 teaspoons salt
- 2 teaspoons pepper
- 4 cups tomatoes, chopped
- 3 tablespoons arrowroot flour

Day of cooking:

- 1 cup chicken stock
- 1 cup coconut milk

Moroccan Lamb Stew

- 4 pounds boneless lamb
- 2 cups onions, chopped
- 2 (15 oz) jars chopped tomatoes, or 4 whole tomatoes, chopped
- 2 cups carrots, chopped
- 1 cup raisins
- 2 teaspoons ground cumin
- 2 teaspoons red pepper flakes
- 1 teaspoon salt
- 2 tablespoons arrowroot flour

Day of cooking:

- 1 cup chicken stock

Please refer to the Assembly section for preparation instructions.

Copyright © 2014 Stephanie Brandt Cornais | Mama & Baby Love
Content may not be reproduced in whole or in part without express written consent.

Prunes and Brandy Lamb Shanks

- 3 pounds of lamb shanks
- 16 pitted prunes
- 4 cups onion, chopped
- 3 cloves garlic, minced
- 1 cup beef stock
- ½ cup full-bodied red wine
- ½ cup brandy
- 2 teaspoons salt
- 2 tablespoon garam masala or curry powder
- 1 teaspoon ground cumin
- 1 teaspoon ground aniseed
- 2 tablespoons arrowroot flour

Day of cooking:
- 1 cup chicken stock

Neapolitan Lamb Stew

- 3 pounds lamb stew meat cut into 1-inch cubes
- 2 (15-ounce) jars of diced tomatoes, or 4 large tomatoes, chopped
- 2 cups onions, chopped
- 1 cup celery, chopped
- 4 cloves garlic, minced
- 1 teaspoon salt
- 1 teaspoon pepper
- 1 tablespoon dried rosemary
- 1 tablespoon dried basil
- 3 tablespoons arrowroot flour

Day of cooking:
- 1 cup red wine

Please refer to the Assembly section for preparation instructions.

Copyright © 2014 Stephanie Brandt Cornais | Mama & Baby Love
Content may not be reproduced in whole or in part without express written consent.

Beef

Beef Curry

2 pounds ground beef

3 cups onion, chopped

1 (15-ounce) jar of diced tomatoes, or 1 large tomato, chopped

1 pound red, russet, or sweet potatoes, peeled and chopped

8 cloves garlic, minced

2 tablespoons curry

2 teaspoons salt

2 teaspoons pepper

2 tablespoons arrowroot flour

Day of cooking:

1 cup filtered water

Peppered Beef Stew

3 pounds of beef stew meat or flank steak

2 cups red onion, thinly sliced

1 pound potatoes, peeled and cubed

1 pound of carrots, peeled and chopped

2 (12-ounce) bottles of gluten free lager beer (sub with beef stock if you prefer)

1 tablespoon Dijon mustard

2 tablespoon Worcestershire sauce

1 teaspoon salt

3 teaspoons pepper, divided

2 tablespoons arrowroot flour

Day of cooking:

1½ cups beef stock

Please refer to the Assembly section for preparation instructions.

Copyright © 2014 Stephanie Brandt Cornais | Mama & Baby Love
Content may not be reproduced in whole or in part without express written consent.

Peach Pot Roast

3 pounds beef stew meat or flank steak

4 cups dried peaches

2 onions, chopped

2 teaspoons all spice

2 teaspoons salt

2 teaspoons pepper

2 tablespoons arrowroot flour

Day of cooking:

2 cups apple juice

Leek Beef Stew

3 pounds of beef stew meat or flank steak

4 cups leeks, chopped, white parts only

1 cup onion, chopped

2 cups carrots, peeled and chopped

3 medium potatoes, peeled and chopped

1 (15-ounce) jar tomato sauce

2 teaspoons black pepper

1 tablespoon dried basil

1 tablespoon dried rosemary

1 tablespoon dried oregano

2 tablespoons arrowroot flour

Day of cooking:

1 cup beef stock

Please refer to the Assembly section for preparation instructions.

Copyright © 2014 Stephanie Brandt Cornais | Mama & Baby Love
Content may not be reproduced in whole or in part without express written consent.

French Dip Beef Stew

- 3 pounds of beef stew meat or flank steak
- 2 pounds whole Portobello mushrooms, chopped, gills removed
- 2 cups onion, thinly sliced
- 2 tablespoons arrowroot flour

Day of cooking:
- 1 cup beef stock

Orange Beef Stew

- 3 pounds of beef stew meat or flank steak
- 1 pound carrots, peeled and chopped
- 8 garlic cloves, minced
- 8 green onions, chopped
- 1 cup onion, chopped
- 2 teaspoons thyme
- 2 teaspoons coriander
- 2 teaspoons cloves
- 2 tablespoons soy sauce
- 1 tablespoon sugar
- 2 tablespoons arrowroot flour

Day of cooking:
- 1 cup orange juice

Please refer to the Assembly section for preparation instructions.

Clementine and Pomegranate Beef Chili

2 pounds ground beef

6 clementines peeled, divided into natural sections

1 cup onion, chopped

4 garlic cloves, minced

1 teaspoon dry mustard

1 teaspoon salt

1 teaspoon pepper

1 teaspoon garlic powder

Day of cooking:

1 cup pomegranate juice

1 cup beef stock

Saint Patrick's Day Stew

3 pounds beef stew meat or flank steak

1 pound potatoes, peeled and chopped

1 pound carrots, peeled and chopped

2 parsnips, chopped

2 cups onions, chopped

6 cloves garlic, minced

2 tablespoons dried thyme, or 6 to 8 fresh springs

½ cup flat-leaf parsley, finely chopped, or 1 tablespoon dried parsley

1 (6-ounce) jar tomato paste

2 tablespoons arrowroot flour

Day of cooking:

2 cups gluten free beer

Please refer to the Assembly section for preparation instructions.

Copyright © 2014 Stephanie Brandt Cornais | Mama & Baby Love
Content may not be reproduced in whole or in part without express written consent.

Herbs de Provence Beef Stew

3 pounds beef stew meat or flank steak

1 pound carrots, peeled chopped

2 onions, chopped

8 garlic cloves, chopped

2 tablespoons arrowroot flour

2 tablespoons of herbs de Provence

1 teaspoon salt

1 teaspoon pepper

Day of cooking:

1 ½ cups beef stock

½ cup of dry red wine

To Make Your Own Herbes de Provence Blend

2 tablespoons dried savory

2 tablespoons dried rosemary

2 tablespoons dried thyme

2 tablespoons dried oregano

2 tablespoons dried basil

2 tablespoons dried marjoram

2 tablespoons dried fennel seed

Please refer to the Assembly section for preparation instructions.

Copyright © 2014 Stephanie Brandt Cornais | Mama & Baby Love
Content may not be reproduced in whole or in part without express written consent.

Beef Stroganoff

- 3 pounds of beef stew meat or flank steak
- 1 pound white mushrooms, sliced
- 1 cup onion, chopped
- 1 cup green onions, chopped
- 2 tablespoons dried parsley
- 1 teaspoon black pepper
- 2 tablespoons dry mustard
- 2 teaspoons honey
- 2 tablespoons tamari sauce
- 4 tablespoons tomato paste
- 4 tablespoons arrowroot powder

Day of Cooking:

- 1 cups beef stock
- 1 cup white wine
- 1 cup sour cream *optional to serve as garnish

Sweet & Hot Flank Steak

- 3 pounds flank steak
- 12 green onions, chopped
- 3 cups bell peppers, any color, chopped
- 6 limes, juiced (zest one of them)
- 1 cup cilantro, chopped
- ½ cup maple syrup
- 2 teaspoons cumin
- 2 teaspoons chili powder
- 1 teaspoon black pepper
- 1 teaspoon salt
- 2 tablespoons arrowroot flour

Day of cooking:

- 1 cup beef stock

Please refer to the Assembly section for preparation instructions.

Pomegranate Beef Stew

3 pounds beef stew meat or flank steak

2 onion, chopped

8 garlic cloves, chopped

4 cups tomatoes, chopped

1 cup golden raisins

2 teaspoons sea salt

2 teaspoons dried rosemary

2 teaspoons dried basil

2 teaspoons dried thyme

2 teaspoons oregano

1 teaspoon cinnamon

¼ cup maple syrup

2 tablespoons arrowroot flour

Day of cooking:

½ cup balsamic vinegar

½ cup beef stock

1 cup unsweetened pomegranate juice

Pumpkin Chili

2 pounds ground beef

2 cups onions, chopped

2 cups red bell peppers, chopped

2 jars (16-ounce) diced tomatoes, or 6 fresh tomatoes, chopped

2 cups tomato sauce

1.5 cups pumpkin puree (a little more than one can of store-bought pumpkin puree)

2 teaspoons chili powder

2 teaspoons cumin

2 teaspoons cinnamon

few drops hot sauce

1 teaspoon salt

1 teaspoon black pepper

Day of cooking:

½ cup filtered water

Please refer to the Assembly section for preparation instructions.

Copyright © 2014 Stephanie Brandt Cornais | Mama & Baby Love
Content may not be reproduced in whole or in part without express written consent.

Italian Beef Stew

3 pounds of beef stew meat or flank steak

3 cups red bell peppers, chopped

8 garlic cloves, minced

2 tablespoons Italian seasoning (homemade version: equal parts basil, marjoram, oregano, rosemary, and thyme)

2 teaspoons red pepper flakes

2 tablespoons arrowroot flour

Day of cooking:

2 cups beef stock

Nut Stew

3 pounds of beef stew meat or flank steak

2 cups onions, chopped

6 cloves garlic, chopped

3 tablespoons fresh ginger, minced

½ head of cabbage, chopped

1 pound potatoes, peeled and chopped

2 (15 oz) jars diced tomatoes with liquid, or 4 whole tomatoes, chopped

2 cups nut butter

2 teaspoons salt

2 teaspoons cayenne pepper

Day of cooking:

2 cups chicken stock

2 cups peas (frozen fine-add the last thirty minutes of cooking)

Please refer to the Assembly section for preparation instructions.

Copyright © 2014 Stephanie Brandt Cornais | Mama & Baby Love
Content may not be reproduced in whole or in part without express written consent.

Stephanie's Goulash

- 3 pounds of beef stew meat or flank steak
- 2 cups onions, chopped
- 2 cups green bell peppers, chopped
- 4 cups beets, peeled and chopped
- 2 cups carrots, peeled and chopped
- 4 cloves garlic, minced
- 2 (6-ounce) jars tomato paste
- 2 tablespoons paprika
- 1 teaspoon ground black pepper
- 2 tablespoons arrowroot flour

Day of cooking:
- ½ cup beef stock
- sour cream for optional garnish

Spicy Beef Taco Filling

- 2 pounds ground beef
- 2 cups onions, minced
- 6 garlic cloves, minced
- 2 teaspoons ground cumin
- 2 teaspoons ground coriander
- 1 teaspoon dried oregano
- 1 (8-ounce) jar of tomato sauce
- 2 teaspoons salt
- 2 teaspoons pepper

Please refer to the Assembly section for preparation instructions.

Copyright © 2014 Stephanie Brandt Cornais | Mama & Baby Love
Content may not be reproduced in whole or in part without express written consent.

Argentine Beef Stew

3 pounds of beef stew meat or flank steak

2 cups scallions, chopped

1 pound potatoes, peeled and chopped

6 cloves garlic, minced

4 tomatoes, chopped

4 tablespoons cilantro, minced

2 teaspoons cumin

2 teaspoons salt

1 teaspoon pepper

2 bay leaves

2 tablespoons arrowroot flour

Day of cooking:

1 cup gluten-free beer

1 cup beef stock

Cumin-Cinnamon Beef Stew

3 pounds beef stew meat or flank steak

2 pounds potatoes

4 cups carrots, peeled and chopped

½ teaspoon chili powder

1½ teaspoons ground cumin

1½ teaspoons cinnamon

½ teaspoon ground coriander

½ teaspoon cayenne pepper

½ teaspoon salt

½ teaspoon black pepper

½ teaspoon of sugar

2 tablespoons arrowroot flour

Day of cooking:

1 cup beef stock

Please refer to the Assembly section for preparation instructions.

Copyright © 2014 Stephanie Brandt Cornais | Mama & Baby Love
Content may not be reproduced in whole or in part without express written consent.

Beef Veggie Soup

3 pounds of beef stew meat or flank steak

4 cups carrots, peeled and chopped

4 cups onions, chopped

1 pound potatoes

4 tomatoes, chopped

2 tablespoons garlic, minced

2 cups peas

2 bay leaves

2 teaspoons dried thyme

2 teaspoons dried parsley

2 tablespoons arrowroot flour

Day of cooking:

2 cups beef stock

Ginger Beef

3 pounds beef stew meat or flank steak

2 cups carrots, peeled and chopped

2 cups scallions, sliced

2 cups red bell pepper, chopped

6 cloves of garlic, minced

4 tablespoons grated fresh ginger

4 tablespoons tamari or gluten-free soy sauce

2 teaspoons red pepper flakes

1 teaspoon salt

1 teaspoon pepper

2 tablespoons arrowroot flour

Day of cooking:

2 cups beef stock

2 cups sugar snap peas (add the last thirty minutes of cooking)

Please refer to the Assembly section for preparation instructions.

Copyright © 2014 Stephanie Brandt Cornais | Mama & Baby Love
Content may not be reproduced in whole or in part without express written consent.

Flank Steak Fajitas

3 pounds flank steak

3 cups onions, chopped

3 cups green bell peppers, chopped

6 cloves garlic, minced

2 (8-ounce) jars of diced tomatoes, or 4 whole tomatoes chopped

2 teaspoons chili powder

2 teaspoons cumin

2 teaspoons coriander

1 teaspoon salt

Day of cooking

½ cup beef stock

lime juice * optional for garnish

Spicy Sweet Potato Beef Stew

3 pounds beef stew meat or flank steak

1 (6-ounce) jar of tomato paste

2 pounds sweet potatoes, peeled and chopped

2 cups butternut squash, chopped

2 celery ribs, chopped

6 garlic cloves, minced

2 teaspoons chili powder

1 teaspoons paprika

1 teaspoon dried thyme

2 teaspoons salt

2 teaspoons black pepper

3 tablespoons arrowroot powder

Day of cooking:

2 cups beef stock

Please refer to the Assembly section for preparation instructions.

Copyright © 2014 Stephanie Brandt Cornais | Mama & Baby Love
Content may not be reproduced in whole or in part without express written consent.

Dijon Beef Roast

3 pounds beef roast or flank steak

½ cup Dijon mustard

1 teaspoon salt

1 teaspoon black pepper

2 tablespoons arrowroot flour

Day of cooking:

1 cup beef stock

Sweet and Sour Brisket

3 pounds beef brisket

4 cups onion, chopped

2 cups carrots, chopped

1 cup celery, chopped

4 cloves garlic, minced

¼ cup sugar

½ cup ketchup

1 teaspoon salt

1 teaspoon pepper

Day of cooking:

1 cup beef stock

6 tablespoons apple cider vinegar

Burgundy Beef

3 pounds of beef stew meat or flank steak

20 baby white onions

1 pound button mushrooms

2 cloves garlic, chopped

2 teaspoons thyme

2 bay leaves

1 teaspoon salt

4 tablespoons arrowroot powder

Day of cooking:

2 cups red wine

Please refer to the Assembly section for preparation instructions.

Chicken

Chicken Tarragon with Leeks

3 pounds chicken

1 pound potatoes

3 leeks (white and light green parts only), halved lengthwise, rinsed, and cut into 1½-inch pieces

1 pound snow peas (added in last 30 minutes of cooking)

1 teaspoon sea salt

1 tablespoon dried tarragon

2 tablespoons arrowroot flour

Day of cooking:

1 cup dry white wine

1 cup chicken stock

Citrus Chicken

3 pounds chicken

2 pounds carrots

2 teaspoons sage

4 tablespoons fresh ginger, peeled and minced or 4 teaspoons of ground ginger

2 tablespoons soy sauce

8 cloves garlic, minced

a few drops of hot sauce

2 tablspoons arrowroot flour

Day of cooking:

1 cup orange juice

1 cup lemon juice

Please refer to the Assembly section for preparation instructions.

Copyright © 2014 Stephanie Brandt Cornais | Mama & Baby Love
Content may not be reproduced in whole or in part without express written consent.

Lemon Chicken

3 pounds chicken

1 pound potatoes, peeled and chopped

5 garlic cloves, peeled and minced

1 lemon, washed well, cut into wedges

6 fresh thyme sprigs (or 1 tablespoon dried thyme)

1 teaspoon sea salt

1 teaspoon arrowroot powder

Day of cooking:

1 cups chicken stock

Chicken and Rhubarb

3 pounds chicken

1 pound trimmed rhubarb, chopped

1 cup celery stalks, chopped

1 cup red onion, chopped

½ cup golden raisins

1 teaspoon freshly ginger, peeled and minced

zest of 1 orange

1/4 cup honey

Day of cooking:

½ cup white wine

¼ cup apple cider vinegar

Please refer to the Assembly section for preparation instructions.

Copyright © 2014 Stephanie Brandt Cornais | Mama & Baby Love
Content may not be reproduced in whole or in part without express written consent.

Spicy Carrot and Chicken Stew

3 pounds chicken

2 pounds carrots, peeled and chopped

4 garlic cloves, minced

1 cup golden raisins

1 cup cilantro leaves

½ cup sliced almonds

2 cinnamon sticks or 2 teaspoons dried cinnamon

2 teaspoons ground cumin

2 teaspoons sea salt

2 teaspoons ground pepper

Day of Cooking

2 cups chicken stock

Strawberry Chicken Stew

3 pounds chicken thighs or chicken breasts, cubed

1 pound strawberries, hulled and cut in half

1 pineapple, cubed

1 teaspoon salt

1 teaspoon pepper

8 ounces chili sauce

2 tablespoons honey

2 cups chicken stock

Please refer to the Assembly section for preparation instructions.

Chicken Marsala

- 2 pounds chicken
- 2 pounds mushrooms (any kind)
- 1 cup onion, chopped
- 4 tablespoons garlic
- 1 teaspoon salt
- 1 teaspoon oregano
- 1 tablespoon sugar
- 1 teaspoon red pepper flakes
- ½ cup fresh basil or 2 tablespoons dried basil
- ½ cup fresh parsley or 2 tablespoons dried basil
- 2 tablespoons arrowroot flour

Day of cooking:
- 2 cups marsala wine (or chicken stock)
- 4 tablespoons fresh lemon juice

Mango Salsa Chicken

- 3 pounds chicken
- 5 mangoes, peeled and diced
- 2 cups onions, chopped
- 6 garlic cloves, chopped
- 2 limes, juiced
- 1 to 3 jalapeno peppers, chopped (depending on how much "heat" you want the dish to have)
- 1 teaspoon salt
- 1 teaspoon pepper
- 2 tablespoons arrowroot flour

Day of cooking:
- 1 cup chicken stock

Please refer to the Assembly section for preparation instructions.

Copyright © 2014 Stephanie Brandt Cornais | Mama & Baby Love
Content may not be reproduced in whole or in part without express written consent.

Chicken Pesto

- 3 pounds chicken
- 8 tomatoes, chopped, or 2 (16-ounce) jars chopped tomatoes
- 1 cup onion, chopped
- 2 cups bell peppers, chopped
- 2 cups zucchini/yellow summer squash, chopped
- 4 cups mushrooms, chopped
- 4 cloves garlic
- 10 tablespoons pesto
- 1 teaspoon salt
- 1 teaspoon pepper
- 2 teaspoons dried Italian seasoning
- 2 tablespoons arrowroot flour

Day of cooking:

- 1 cup chicken stock
- parmesan cheese *optional for garnish

Peach Chicken Sweet Potato Stew

- 2 pounds chicken
- 4 cups peaches, quartered and chopped
- 1 pound sweet potatoes, chopped
- 2 cups onions, chopped
- 4 garlic cloves, minced
- 2 teaspoons onion powder
- 2 teaspoons garlic powder
- 1 tablespoon sugar
- 2 teaspoons cinnamon
- ¼ teaspoon seasoned pepper
- 1 teaspoon turmeric
- 1 teaspoon celery salt
- 1 teaspoon parsley
- 2 tablespoons arrowroot flour

Day of cooking:

- 1 cup chicken stock

Please refer to the Assembly section for preparation instructions.

Copyright © 2014 Stephanie Brandt Cornais | Mama & Baby Love
Content may not be reproduced in whole or in part without express written consent.

Tex Mex Shredded Chicken

3 pounds skinless, boneless chicken breasts

2 chili peppers (haberno or jalepeno), finely chopped

4 cups bell peppers, sliced

2 cups red onion, chopped

8 garlic cloves, minced

¼ cup cilantro, minced

4 tablespoons Worcestershire sauce

3 teaspoons honey

Day of cooking:

1 cup chicken stock

1/2 cup lime juice

Chicken Rosemary and Apple Stew

3 pounds chicken

2 cups onions, chopped

1 pound apples, peeled, cored and chopped (Braeburn or Fuji work best)

6 garlic cloves, minced

2 lemons, juiced

1 teaspoon salt

1 teaspoon pepper

2 teaspoons dried rosemary leaves

2 tablespoons arrowroot flour

Day of cooking:

1 cup of chicken stock

Please refer to the Assembly section for preparation instructions.

Copyright © 2014 Stephanie Brandt Cornais | Mama & Baby Love
Content may not be reproduced in whole or in part without express written consent.

Honey Apple Chicken

3 pounds chicken

1 pound apples, peeled, cored, and chopped (Braeburn or Fuji work best)

1 cup red bell pepper, chopped

2 bunches of green onions, chopped

6 tablespoons honey

2 teaspoons salt

2 teaspoons ground black pepper

2 tablespoons arrowroot flour

Day of cooking:

½ cup apple cider or (unsweetened apple juice)

1 cup chicken stock

Thai Chicken Curry

3 pounds chicken

2 cups onions, chopped

2 cups red bell peppers, chopped

2 cups green bell peppers, chopped

1 pound potatoes

4 to 6 cloves garlic, finely chopped or grated

2-inch knob ginger, peeled and grated

2 tablespoons curry powder

2 tablespoons sugar

2 tablespoons soy sauce

2 tablespoons arrowroot flour

Day of cooking:

2 cups coconut milk

1 lime, cut into wedges*

2 scallions, thinly sliced*

½ cup chopped cilantro*

½ cup chopped thai basil*

*optional for garnish

Please refer to the Assembly section for preparation instructions.

Healing Chicken Soup

2 cups onions, chopped

1 pound carrots, peeled and chopped

2 cups celery stalks, chopped

2 cups kale, chopped

2 teaspoons salt

1 teaspoon pepper

1 teaspoon basil

1 teaspoon thyme

a couple sprigs of fresh parsley

4 bay leaves

Day of cooking:

1 (2½ pound) whole/fryer chicken

4 cups filtered water

1 tablespoon of apple cider vinegar

Chicken and Cherries

3 pounds of chicken

1.5 pounds cherries (jarred, frozen or fresh)

chili sauce to taste

¼ cup sugar

2 tablespoons arrowroot flour

Day of cooking:

½ cup of chicken stock

Please refer to the Assembly section for preparation instructions.

Copyright © 2014 Stephanie Brandt Cornais | Mama & Baby Love
Content may not be reproduced in whole or in part without express written consent.

Cranberry Chicken

- 3 pounds chicken
- 2 cups apples, cut into wedges
- 2 cups onion, chopped
- 2 (15-ounce) jars of cranberry sauce
- 2 tablespoons honey *if needed
- 2 tablespoons arrowroot flour

Day of cooking:
juice of two lemons

Healthy Mama BBQ Chicken

- 3 pounds chicken
- 1 pound potatoes, peeled and chopped
- 2 cups green bell peppers, chopped
- 1 cup red bell pepper, chopped
- 2 cups zucchini, chopped
- 2 cups onion, chopped
- 2 (15-ounce) jars tomato sauce
- 2 tablespoons sugar
- 2 tablespoons Worcestershire sauce
- 2 tablespoon ground yellow mustard
- 6 cloves garlic finely minced
- 1 teaspoon salt
- 2 tablespoon arrowroot flour

Day of cooking:
½ cup chicken stock

Handwritten note: Split veggies in half - 2 bags. Kept spices at full amount into each bag

Please refer to the Assembly section for preparation instructions.

Copyright © 2014 Stephanie Brandt Cornais | Mama & Baby Love
Content may not be reproduced in whole or in part without express written consent.

Chicken Curry

3 pounds chicken

3 tablespoons curry powder

2 teaspoons ground cumin

2 cups potatoes, peeled and chopped

2 cups carrots, peeled and chopped

4 cups mango, chopped

1 cup onion, chopped

1 cup zucchini, chopped

2 cloves garlic, minced

2 bay leaves

1 teaspoon thyme

1 teaspoon coriander

1 teaspoon cloves

2 tablespoons arrowroot flour

Add day of cooking:

½ cup chicken stock

½ cup raisins *optional for garnish

½ cup cashews *optional for garnish

Chicken Chili

3 pounds chicken breasts

2 pounds potatoes

2 (6-ounce) jars tomato paste

2 (15-ounce) jars of diced tomatoes, or 2 whole tomatoes chopped

1 tablespoon of chili powder

1 teaspoon garlic powder

1 teaspoon onion powder

1 teaspoon red pepper flakes

1 teaspoon oregano

1 teaspoon paprika

2 teaspoons cumin

1 teaspoon salt

1 teaspoon pepper

Please refer to the Assembly section for preparation instructions.

Copyright © 2014 Stephanie Brandt Cornais | Mama & Baby Love
Content may not be reproduced in whole or in part without express written consent.

Chicken and Cauliflower Masala

- 3 pounds chicken
- 2 pounds potatoes
- 1 large cauliflower, trimmed and broken into 2-inch pieces
- 1 (15-ounce) jar of diced tomatoes, or 1 large tomato, chopped
- 1 teaspoon ground turmeric
- 2 teaspoons ground coriander
- 1 teaspoon garam masala
- 1 teaspoon sugar
- 1 teaspoon salt
- 1 jalapeno pepper, stemmed, seeded, and finely chopped (*optional for more spice)
- 2 tablespoon arrowroot flour

Day of cooking:

- 1 lime, juiced
- ½ cup chicken stock
- 3 tablespoons of fresh cilantro *optional for garnish

Asian Ginger Chicken

- 3 pounds chicken
- 1 cup onion, chopped
- 4 tablespoons fresh ginger, peeled and minced
- 3 tablespoons gluten-free tamari or soy sauce
- 1 tablespoon sugar
- 1 bunch of scallions, chopped
- 1 teaspoon salt
- 1 teaspoon pepper
- 3 tablespoons arrowroot powder

Day of cooking:

- 1 cup chicken stock

Please refer to the Assembly section for preparation instructions.

Copyright © 2014 Stephanie Brandt Cornais | Mama & Baby Love
Content may not be reproduced in whole or in part without express written consent.

Polynesian Chicken

3 pounds chicken breasts, thighs, or bone-in pieces

3 cups red pepper, chopped

1 whole pineapple (about 3 cups), chopped

6 cloves garlic, minced

4 tablespoons ginger, peeled, and minced

1 cup honey

4 tablespoons soy sauce

3 tablespoons arrowroot powder

1 teaspoon salt

1 teaspoon pepper

Day of cooking

½ cup chicken stock

Cilantro Lime Chicken

3 pounds of chicken

2 tablespoons shredded lime zest

1 teaspoon salt

1 teaspoon pepper

2 teaspoons garlic powder

2 tablespoons of arrowroot flour

Day of cooking:

4 tablespoons lime juice

1 cup chicken stock

2 cups fresh cilantro, chopped (*add the last 30 minutes of cooking)

parmesan cheese, or nutritional yeast for dairy free

*optional for garnish

Please refer to the Assembly section for preparation instructions.

Copyright © 2014 Stephanie Brandt Cornais | Mama & Baby Love
Content may not be reproduced in whole or in part without express written consent.

Fennel, Artichoke, and Chicken Stew

- 3 pounds of chicken
- 2 fennel bulbs, stems, and leaves trimmed and bulbs cut lengthwise into ½-inch thick slices
- 1 cup onion, chopped
- 1 tomato, chopped
- 1 (15-ounce) jar of artichoke hearts, drained and chopped
- 1 teaspoon dried rosemary
- 1 teaspoon dried oregano
- 1 teaspoon dried thyme
- 1 teaspoon salt
- 1 teaspoon pepper
- 1 tablespoon arrowroot flour

Day of cooking:
- ½ dry white wine
- ½ cup chicken stock

Pineapple Teriyaki Chicken

- 3 pounds chicken drumsticks
- 1 whole pineapple, chopped (frozen is fine too)
- ¼ cup soy sauce
- ¼ cup hoisin sauce

Day of cooking:
- ½ cup of chicken stock

Please refer to the Assembly section for preparation instructions.

Copyright © 2014 Stephanie Brandt Cornais | Mama & Baby Love
Content may not be reproduced in whole or in part without express written consent.

Apricot Chicken

- 3 pounds of chicken
- 2 cups dried apricots
- 3 cups onion, chopped
- 2 cloves garlic, chopped
- 2 tablespoons fresh ginger, peeled and minced
- 1 (15-ounce) jar of diced tomatoes, or 1 large tomato, chopped
- 2 teaspoons salt
- 1 pinch saffron

Day of cooking:
- 1 cup chicken stock

Tarragon Chicken

- 3 pounds of chicken
- 1 pound potatoes, peeled and chopped
- 1 pound carrots, peeled and chopped
- 2 cups onion, chopped
- 1 teaspoon salt
- 6 springs fresh tarragon, or 1 tablespoon dried
- 2 tablespoons arrowroot powder

Day of cooking:
- 1 cup dry white wine
- 1 cup chicken stock

Please refer to the Assembly section for preparation instructions.

Copyright © 2014 Stephanie Brandt Cornais | Mama & Baby Love
Content may not be reproduced in whole or in part without express written consent.

Jerk Chicken

3 pounds of chicken

1 bunch scallions, chopped

2 habanero or jalepeno chilies, stemmed and seeded

2 tablespoons fresh ginger, peeled and minced

3 garlic cloves, minced

2 tablespoons honey

1 tablespoon dried thyme

2 teaspoons ground allspice

1 teaspoon salt

Day of cooking:

juice of 1 lime

½ cup chicken stock

Shredded Chicken

3 pounds chicken breast

3 cups onion, chopped

3 cups green bell peppers, chopped

6 garlic cloves, minced

2 (15-ounce) jars of diced tomatoes, or 6 large tomatoes, chopped

3 tablespoons tomato paste

1 teaspoon salt

1 teaspoon chili powder

1 teaspoon pepper

1 tablespoon paprika

1 tablespoon cumin

1 teaspoon oregano

Day of cooking:

1 cup chicken stock

Please refer to the Assembly section for preparation instructions.

Copyright © 2014 Stephanie Brandt Cornais | Mama & Baby Love
Content may not be reproduced in whole or in part without express written consent.

Pork

Pork and Grapes

3 pounds of pork

4 tablespoons shallots, minced

2 cups grapes, cut in half (red or green)

2 tablespoons tarragon, fresh or dried

1 teaspoon salt

1 teaspoon pepper

2 teaspoons sugar

1 tablespoon Dijon mustard

3 tablespoons arrowroot flour

Day of cooking:

4 tablespoons red wine

1 cup chicken stock

Apple Pie Pork Chops

3 pounds pork chops

6 cups apples, sliced and peeled

3 tablespoons maple syrup

2 teaspoons cinnamon

2 teaspoons cloves

2 teaspoons allspice

2 tablespoons arrowroot powder

Day of cooking:

1 cup filtered water

Please refer to the Assembly section for preparation instructions.

Copyright © 2014 Stephanie Brandt Cornais | Mama & Baby Love
Content may not be reproduced in whole or in part without express written consent.

Cranberry Orange Pork Roast

- 3 pounds pork loin roast
- 1 cup dried cranberries
- 2 cups homemade cranberry sauce, or 1 (15-ounce) jar of cranberry sauce
- 2 tablespoons orange zest
- 2 teaspoons nutmeg
- 2 teaspoons cloves
- 1 teaspoon cinnamon
- 1 teaspoon salt
- 1 teaspoon pepper
- 2 tablespoons arrowroot flour

Day of cooking:

- 1 cup orange juice

Blueberry Balsamic Ribs

- 3 pounds boneless pork ribs
- 2 cups blueberries, mashed
- 2 cloves garlic, minced
- 2 shallots, minced
- 1 tablespoon fresh ginger, minced, or 1 teaspoon powdered
- ½ teaspoon jalapeno, seeded and minced
- 2 tablespoons sugar
- 2 teaspoons ground chipotle
- ½ teaspoon paprika
- 1 teaspoon salt
- 1 teaspoon ground black pepper
- 2 tablespoons balsamic vinegar
- 2 teaspoons Worcestershire sauce
- ½ cup of beef stock
- ¾ cup hot sauce

Please refer to the Assembly section for preparation instructions.

Copyright © 2014 Stephanie Brandt Cornais | Mama & Baby Love
Content may not be reproduced in whole or in part without express written consent.

made w/ TJ Italian Sausage Links + Russian Kale

Sausage and Kale Soup

3 pounds sausage

4 cups kale, ripped into small pieces with stems and spines removed

10 garlic cloves, minced

1 cup onion, chopped

2 teaspoons basil

2 teaspoons marjoram

2 teaspoons oregano

2 teaspoons rosemary

2 teaspoons thyme

~~1 teaspoon salt~~ *way too salty!*

1 teaspoon pepper

2 teaspoon parsley

Day of cooking:

2 cups chicken stock *– not nearly enough*

4
6

Plum Sauce Pork Chops

3 pounds pork chops

3 pounds plums, pitted and cut in half

1 cup sweet onion, chopped

1 teaspoon fresh ginger, peeled and minced

1 clove garlic, peeled and minced

¼ cup sugar

1 teaspoon ground coriander

1 teaspoon salt

1 teaspoon cinnamon

½ teaspoon cayenne pepper

½ teaspoon ground cloves

2 tablespoons arrowroot flour

Day of cooking:

½ cup apple cider vinegar

½ cup chicken stock

Please refer to the Assembly section for preparation instructions.

Copyright © 2014 Stephanie Brandt Cornais | Mama & Baby Love
Content may not be reproduced in whole or in part without express written consent.

Mango Pork

- 3 pounds pork
- 2 mangos, chopped
- 4 garlic cloves, minced
- 1 tomato, chopped
- 1 teaspoon salt
- 1 teaspoon pepper
- 1 teaspoons ground chipotle
- 1 teaspoon chili powder
- ½ teaspoon oregano
- 2 tablespoons arrowroot flour

Day of cooking:
- ½ cup orange juice
- ½ cup lime juice

Sausage and Tomato Ragu

- 3 pounds Italian sausage cut in 2-inch pieces
- 3 cups onions, chopped
- 1 cup celery ribs, chopped
- 2 cups carrots, chopped
- 4 cloves garlic, minced
- 2 (15-ounce) jar of diced tomatoes, or 1 large tomato, chopped
- 1 (15-ounce) jar of tomato sauce
- 1 tablespoon of dried rosemary
- 1 teaspoon of allspice
- 1 teaspoon salt
- 1 teaspoon ground pepper
- 2 tablespoons of arrowroot flour

Day of cooking:
- 1 cup beef stock
- 1 cup red wine

Please refer to the Assembly section for preparation instructions.

Copyright © 2014 Stephanie Brandt Cornais | Mama & Baby Love
Content may not be reproduced in whole or in part without express written consent.

Jerk Pork and Sweet Potatoes

3 pounds pork ribs

2 pounds sweet potatoes, peeled and chopped

1 bunch of scallions, chopped

1 (15-ounce) jar of diced tomatoes, or 1 large tomato, chopped

1 haberno or jalapeno pepper, stemmed, seeded and minced

4 cloves garlic, minced

1 teaspoon dried thyme

2 teaspoons ground allspice

2 teaspoons salt

1 teaspoon pepper

3 tablespoons sugar

2 tablespoons arrowroot flour

Day of cooking:

1 cup chicken stock

Yummy Shredded Pork

3 pounds pork

2 cups onion, chopped

1 (15-ounce) jar of tomato sauce

1 jarred chipotle chili, minced

6 cloves garlic, minced

¼ cup chili powder

1 tablespoon ground coriander

1 tablespoon ground cumin

1 teaspoon salt

1 teaspoon pepper

2 teaspoons sugar

Day of cooking:

½ cup of chicken stock

juice of 1 lime

*needs to be cooked longer than 8 hours to fall apart and shred

Please refer to the Assembly section for preparation instructions.

Copyright © 2014 Stephanie Brandt Cornais | Mama & Baby Love
Content may not be reproduced in whole or in part without express written consent.

Honey Mustard Pork Roast

3 pounds pork

½ cup honey

1 cup Dijon mustard

1 tablespoon sugar

1 teaspoon salt

1 teaspoon pepper

1 teaspoon garlic powder

1 teaspoon onion powder

2 tablespoons arrowroot flour

Day of cooking:

½ cup chicken stock

Ginger-Cranberry Pork Roast

3 pounds pork loin roast

2 (15-ounce) jar of cranberry sauce

1 cup fresh ginger, peeled and minced

2 tablespoons sugar

1 teaspoon salt

2 tablespoons arrowroot flour

Day of cooking:

1 cup filtered water

Please refer to the Assembly section for preparation instructions.

Pork and Prunes Stew

- 3 pounds pork
- 2 cups pitted prunes
- 3 cups onion, chopped
- 1 teaspoon salt
- 2 teaspoons dried thyme
- 2 bay leaves
- 3 tablespoons arrowroot flour

Day of cooking:
- 1 cup chicken stock
- 1 cup hard cider or white wine

Harvest Pork Roast

- 3 pork
- 2 pounds carrots, chopped
- 1 pound parsnips, chopped
- 2 cups green peppers, chopped
- 2 cups celery, chopped
- 2 teaspoons cinnamon
- 2 teaspoons black pepper
- 2 teaspoons salt
- 4 tablespoons arrowroot flour

Day of cooking:
- 1 cup apple cider
- 1 cup beef stock

Please refer to the Assembly section for preparation instructions.

Thanks for reading!

As the Founder and Creative Director of Mama and Baby Love—once a yoga studio and eco-friendly boutique and now a thriving website about Real Food, natural living, motherhood, and healing—I thank you for purchasing and using my cookbook.

As a mother, healer, mentor, and businesswoman, I care deeply about nourishing and loving myself so that I can nourish and love my family. It means so much to me to be able to share helpful information with other mothers. I truly hope the recipes in this cookbook help you nourish and love yourself and your own families, and help you on your journey to being the healthiest, happiest mother you can be. These recipes and this way of cooking have changed my life and I am so excited for you to experience that, too.

You can learn more about here, sign up for my email newsletter here (and get three free ebooks about motherhood and healthy living), subscribe to my podcast show and YouTube channel and I would love to connect with you on social media, too. You can find me on Google+, Instagram, Twitter, Pinterest, and Facebook. I look forward to connecting and working with you!

You may also be interested in:

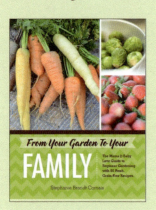

From Your Garden to Your Family

M+BL's Gluten-Free Grain-Free Baking

From Your Garden To Your FAMILY

The Mama & Baby Love Guide to Beginner Gardening with 50 Fresh, Grain-Free Recipes.

Stephanie Brandt Cornais

**From Your Garden To Your Family:
The Mama and Baby Love Guide to
Beginner Gardening with 50 Fresh, Grain-Free Recipes.**

Copyright 2014 by Nourish + Love, LLC. All rights reserved. No part of this publication may be reproduced or transmitted in any form or by any means, electronic or mechanical, including photocopying, recording or by any information storage and retrieval system, without permission in writing from the Publisher.

Inquiries or requests to the Publisher for permission should be addressed to:

Stephanie Brandt Cornais
4300 South US HWY #1 Ste 203-132
Jupiter, Florida 33477

info@MamaAndBabyLove.com

Produced by Nourish + Love, LLC
Recipes by Stephanie Brandt Cornais
Photographs by Stephanie Brandt Cornais and Lisa Waszkiewicz

Content Editor: Scott Sweeney
Copy Editor: Leslee Boldman
Nutrition Editor: Cassandra Roy
Designed by Mackenzie Miller, Pop! Creative Design

chapter outline

My Gardening Story 1
Building a Backyard Garden 3
Starting an Herb Garden 4
Gardening by the Moon 5
Seasons and Food 9

WINTER
    Leeks 9
    Beets 12
    Citrus 13
    Rhubarb 14
    Greens 16
    Brussels Sprouts 19

SPRING
    Radishes 20
    Peas 22
    Carrots 23
    Strawberries 24
    Chard 25
    Mushrooms 27
    Mangoes 29

SUMMER
    Zucchini/Squash 31
    Blueberries 34
    Tomatoes 36
    Watermelon 39
    Figs 40
    Peaches 41
    Eggplant 42

FALL
    Okra 44
    Bell Peppers 45
    Grapes 46
    Apples 48
    Pomegranates 49
    Pumpkins 50
    Cranberries 53

My Gardening Story

Gardening has been a peaceful and healing hobby of mine for a long time. I first started gardening when I was about 10 years old, growing radishes and sunflowers in a little spot in my yard. I could not believe that so much could come of a tiny seed. I actually come from a long line of farmers. Some day, when I realize my dream of moving past being a backyard gardener and having my own farm, I will be a 4th-generation farmer.

When I garden, I not only feel a connection to the earth and seasons, but also to my ancestors. Whether or not there are farmers in your family lineage, we all have great-grandparents who at least had a small backyard garden. Our ancestors were hunters and gathers, and even if we have forgotten this part of ourselves, gardening is a huge part of the collective human experience and consciousness.

I love that gardening is becoming popular again and that we as a society are returning to our roots, beginning to care once more for where our food comes from and about the quality of what we eat. A homegrown green pepper not only tastes better but is less toxic and contains more vitamins and nutrients.

Gardening is also great exercise and something fun to do with the kids. The garden is a great excuse to get outside and do something relaxing. Plus, "Let's go check on the vegetables!" is a great way to redirect your kids away from a meltdown. The vegetables a child helps grow and harvest are much more likely to be eaten. I am convinced that the biggest reason my daughter Penelope—even with her Sensory Processing Disorder that makes her a much pickier than the average child—eats the vegetables she does, is because of her early and consistent experiences with gardening and growing her own food.

Also, it's incredibly helpful to get to know your local farmers. They have a wealth of information and will be excited to share their knowledge and tips with you. Some farms may even have classes for the community. It's a safe bet that if you strike up

Start small.
Get a big pot for a cherry tomato plant or some arugula in the fall, which is an easier time for a beginner because there are less bugs and pests to deal with.

a conversation with a farmer at the farmers' market, they will talk your ear off and tell you everything you need to know about growing a specific fruit or vegetable in your area. This is how I learned most of what I know about gardening and it is the easiest way to begin. I learn best when I am talking to someone face to face and then just diving in and getting involved.

I encourage you to start gardening. Start small. Get a big pot for a cherry tomato plant or some arugula in the fall, which is an easier time for a beginner because there are less bugs and pests to deal with. Gardening has a learning curve and it is a life-long education. I am not a master and I probably will learn something new about gardening until the day I die. Even farmers who have been growing food their whole lives will have an off season of a particular plant for no apparent reason at all; knowing this, I hope you will feel less like a failure.

To get started with *gardening*, you need to **move past the fear of failure.**

I view gardening as a huge experiment and try to not have any expectations of how a crop will do. I have held this attitude from the very beginning. At first, it was because I wasn't going to let my inexperience stop me from learning. Then I quickly realized that even the most experienced farmers can't predict what is going to happen. Some time, that basil crop is just going to suck and there is nothing you could have done to change that.

To get started with gardening, you need to move past the fear of failure, let go of old thought patterns about yourself, the stories you tell about your black thumb. Get excited about every little success and let the failures slip away. Keep working at it, and eventually you will learn how to garden, you will grow yourself a green thumb, I guarantee it.

Building a Backyard Garden

Raised beds are a great option for an urban garden. They really help plants thrive because of the excellent drainage and increased control over the soil. I chose raised beds in our yard for several reasons:

1. They look neat and tidy. Y'all know what an OCD, organized nut I am. Everything in my home needs a place and some sort of physical way to be contained. My garden is no different. In Tallahassee, I had a 10 x 30 foot garden that was contained by cement blocks. In Jupiter, I have premade, raised garden beds, including a 4 x 8 contraption called a GrowCamp and two smaller Mini Farm Boxes—cedar beds on rollers both from the amazing company, Earth Easy.

2. The raised beds make it a lot easier to have kids in the garden. It's a clear delineation of what part of the yard is for playing and what part is for growing food. It helped keep our dog, Sky, out of the garden, too.

3. It's easier to weed. With raised beds, the soil tends to be looser and easier to pull up weeds. It's also a bit less taxing on your back, although part of what makes gardening good exercise is the bending down and standing up—essentially the same movement you will pay a personal trainer to tell you to do! (Side note: I also like to squat a lot when I am gardening, which is the most important yoga pose a female woman can do for her health.)

4. Raised beds provide good drainage. This is crucial where I live now, as the afternoon rain just dumps buckets.

How to build wood raised beds:

MATERIALS

Three 8-foot 2×6's

Twelve 3 1/2-inch screws or nails

Old cardboard boxes free of staples, tape, etc.

Topsoil, compost, etc. (Most garden-supply centers and home-improvement stores will sell topsoil in large quantities and will even deliver. Compost will provide the most nutrients but may be too expensive to buy in large quantities.)

Cut one of the boards into two equal pieces (two 4-foot boards). Make a rectangle with your two 4-foot boards and the two remaining 8-foot boards and connect with three screws at each corner. Position the rectangle where you want your bed. (The resulting structure can get heavy, so it's best to built it near or even exactly where you'll want it.) Lay down the cardboard to cover any grass or weeds. Cover the cardboard with topsoil. If you're only going to be growing lettuce and other leafy greens, the soil doesn't need to be too deep. But if you have an inexpensive supply of soil or compost, go ahead and lay it on thick. The cardboard will ensure weeds don't grow up from below.

We chose 4 x 8 simply because it's a manageable space. If your garden is much wider, you'll have trouble reaching across to pick fruit or pull weeds.

Our beds are 6 inches tall, which is relatively short for raised beds. But we knew we wouldn't be adding a whole lot of soil to begin with, so there wasn't much point in making them taller.

You can also use cement blocks, which is much easier but not as pretty.

Starting an Herb Garden

I think starting a small herb garden is a great way to get your toe wet. In Tallahassee, I had a separate 5 x 8 herb garden that was right off my back porch, giving me easy access while prepping meals. In Jupiter, I am using Mini Farm Boxes on my porch as my herb garden. Here is a quick rundown of the types of herbs, whether they are perennials or annuals, and what kind of cooking they are good for.

PERENNIALS
(Come back for multiple years without replanting)

Sage: It is so delicious, especially paired with sausage or squash. Or you can dry it and burn it to clear the energy in your home!

Oregano: Great in tomato sauces and Italian food in general.

Rosemary: Such an easy herb to grow, and they grow big! Rosemary was the first thing I planted when we bought our house in Tallahassee, and when we moved out 8 years later, it was 4 feet wide and 5 feet tall! Roast some potatoes with Rosemary for an easy side dish and it will also make your house smell incredible.

Thyme: Add sprigs of fresh Sage, Oregano, Thyme, and Rosemary to the pot when you're making chicken stock to give it a rich and yummy flavor.

Peppermint: Great for teas and desserts.

ANNUALS (Must be planted each year)

Basil: This summer-thriving herb is a must for Italian or Thai dishes. And when you are overflowing with end-of-the-summer basil, you can always make pesto and freeze it for a later date.

Dill: I love the combination of lemon and dill! It's a lifesaver when I realize late in the afternoon that I never planned dinner and the fresh dill makes a last-minute tuna salad taste heavenly. Especially if you have some green onions to add!

Parsley: If there's an herb that's good in everything, this is it. We use it all the time! It's hugely detoxifying, and a great added green in kale green smoothies.

Cilantro: So delicious and a necessity in various kinds of ethnic dishes, like guacamole or spring rolls. And like parsley, add cilantro to your green smoothie for extra detoxification.

I usually plant two to three of each herb and that is enough for my cooking needs. However, I usually do a full crop of basil (six to eight plants) because I love to make huge batches of pesto and freeze it for later.

Gardening by the Moon

Planting with the moon cycle in mind is a cool way to really get in touch with Mother Nature and experience the energy, vibrations, and wisdom of the earth. I feel that gardening in this way has helped me become aware of my own cycles and rhythms, and even be more in touch with my emotions. This is a way for me to feel connected to everything around me.

It also helps your plants grow better. Honestly, I am not smarty pants enough to explain why. I just took my favorite gardener/yogi master's word and never really looked into it, but when you correctly plant according to the moon's phases, your overall plants' health is better and the harvest is more bountiful. If you need a more scientific explanation, just Google "moisture content in soil during the new and full moon."

I have been gardening by the moon since I started. I don't always get it right; sometimes life is so full that I am happy just to get the damn plants in the ground, regardless of where the heck the moon is in the sky. If I miss the proper moon window, I will still plant. I always plant. Do the best you can to get in touch with the moon's cycle, but don't let your concern that it's not the perfect moon time keep you from planting your garden. It will still grow.

In general, you want to plant root crops when the moon is decreasing/waning (getting smaller after a full moon), and plant aboveground crops when the moon is increasing/waxing (growing larger toward a full moon). You will want to get your hands on a local (specific to your zone) moon cycle calendar because there are also very specific days to transfer baby plants and to directly sow seeds, and then there are even specific times of the moon cycle to kill plant pests and weed. You can usually find these at a farmers' market or feed store.

> " To everything there is a season, and a time for every purpose, a time to be born, a time to die, a time to plant and a time to pluck up that which was planted.
> —Ecclesiastes 3 "

Here are some general, yearly moon cycles you can follow for what types of plants/species to plant during the year:

1st Quarter

During the 1st quarter of the moon, you should plant asparagus, barley, broccoli, Brussels sprouts, cabbage, cress, endive, kohlrabi, leek, lettuce, oats, onions, parsley, spinach, and seeds of flowering plants.

2nd Quarter

During the 2nd quarter of the moon, you should plant beans, eggplant, peas, peppers, pumpkin, squash, tomatoes, and watermelon.

3rd Quarter

During the 3rd quarter of the moon, you should plant artichoke, beets, carrots, chicory, parsnips, potatoes, radish, rutabaga, turnip, and all bulbous flowering plants.

4th Quarter

During the 4th quarter of the moon, you should turn sod, pull weeds, destroy noxious growth, and cover beds.

Seasons and Foods

Obviously, if you are gardening in your backyard, you are eating the fruit of your labor and, thus, naturally eating in-season foods. But until you get to a point where your garden is meeting all your family's fruit and vegetable needs, there are so many benefits to buying food in season from local farmers and the grocery store.

Surely, you have had a tasteless tomato or strawberry during the off season and know what I am talking about. Forcing nature is never a good idea. When you pick a veggie or fruit before it is ripe to accommodate shipping logistics, taste gets compromised.

When you buy produce in season, not only are you supporting your local farmer and getting the most nutritious food in your body (in-season vegetables have more vitamins and nutrients!), but it is also healthier for the earth. Buying food that has the least amount of distance to ship reduces our carbon footprint. Global warming is no joke.

Buying produce in season helps me feel connected to the earth and its seasons. I feel grounded and present and connected in this life by noticing the changes in routine that each season brings. By following what is available to eat each season, I feel alive and in the moment.

In-season produce is at the cheapest price you will find all year long, even at the grocery store. If you stock up and freeze/can/ferment/dehydrate produce while it is season, you will save a ton of money.

And I also just like supporting small farmers, not just because I am supporting the local economy when I do that, but I liken modern, non-industrialized farmers to healers. These days, anyone who feels a calling to be a farmer, and who treats their land and animals with love and respect, is doing a huge service to not only me, the end consumer, but to entire world. To me, they are answering God's call to be of Service to Him. I think they are spiritual warriors, sacrificing and leading the way to restore balance to the earth and system.

So, what's in season? As far as when vegetables and fruits are in season and ready to harvest, this book provides general information. I can't get too specific for every region of the world, but this is a good guide for North America to get you started.

A simple Internet search will help you narrow down exactly what is in season in your specific area. Better yet, talk to local farmers at the farmers' market. These days, most farms have newsletters that not only tell you what is in season to harvest, but also information on planting for home gardeners. So if I list rhubarb as in season for January, it's in

Why buy local?

1 **Eating local and in season is good for you and tastes better, too.** Locally grown food doesn't travel far, so farmers can choose varieties based on flavor, rather than their ability to withstand a long journey.

2 **It is good for the economy.** The money you spend on local food stays in the area, as it supports the work of local farmers and markets.

3 **It is good for the environment.** The average American meal travels nearly 1,500 miles before reaching the plate. When you eat local food, you reduce the consumption of fossil fuels, carbon dioxide emissions, and wasteful packing material.

4 **It is good for family farms.** With each local purchase, you ensure more of the money spent goes to a local farmer.

> **Buy in-season.**
> In-season produce is at the cheapest price you will find all year long, even at the grocery store. If you stock up and freeze/can/ferment/dehydrate produce while it is in season, you will save a ton of money.

season in the Southeastern U.S. and may not be in your area. This book is a perfect introduction to help you figure out general times when produce is in season and give you the foundation to understanding the flow of the growing seasons in your specific microclimate.

The same goes for the recipes and gardening info in this cookbook. I have used my general locale to list what is in season each month. When I first started writing this book, I lived in North Florida, very close to Georgia (Zone 8a) where we would get several good-length freezes each year, sometimes even a flutter of snow. In that area, there was an amazingly large variety of produce that I could grow or buy from farms within a 250-mile radius. Now I live in South Florida (Zone 10a), and my seasons are all pretty much turned on their head because winter is the main growing season here. I have a lot of new tropical and subtropical things I can grow now, but I also lost a few of my favorites crops that don't grow well in South Florida.

On the following page is a general listing of what vegetables and fruit are in season each month.

Planting Calendar

DECEMBER
Vegetables: artichokes, beets, broccoli, Brussels sprouts, cabbage, cauliflower, celery, celery root, chanterelle mushrooms, greens, parsnips, rutabagas, turnips, winter squash

Fruit: apples, blood oranges, coconuts, dates, grapefruit, grapes, kiwi, pears, persimmons, pomegranates, tangerines

JANUARY
Vegetables: avocados, beets, broccoli, Brussels sprouts, cabbage, cauliflower, celery, celery root, chanterelle mushrooms, greens, parsnips, rutabagas, turnips

Fruit: apples, blood oranges, dates, grapefruit, kiwi, lemons, limes, papayas, pears, pomelos, tangerines

FEBRUARY
Vegetables: avocados, Brussels sprouts, cabbage, celery, celery root, chanterelle mushrooms, greens, parsnips, rutabagas, turnips

Fruit: apples, dates, grapefruit, kiwi, lemons, limes, oranges, papayas, pomelos, tangerines

winter

MARCH
Vegetables: asparagus, beets, corn, green beans, peas, peppers

Fruit: bananas, berries, figs, kiwi, mangos, pineapple

APRIL
Vegetables: artichokes, asparagus, green beans, beets, corn, fava beans, fiddlehead ferns, peas, peppers

Fruit: bananas, berries, figs, kiwi, mangoes, nectarines, peaches, pineapple, plums

MAY
Vegetables: artichokes, asparagus, green beans, beets, corn, fava beans, kohlrabi, peas, peppers, spinach

Fruit: apricots, bananas, cherries, figs, mangoes, melons, nectarines, peaches, pineapples, plums

spring

JUNE
Vegetables: asparagus, beets, corn, fava beans, green beans, kohlrabi, peas, peppers, spinach

Fruit: apricots, bananas, berries, cherries, mangoes, melons, peaches, pineapple, plums

JULY
Vegetables: avocados, beets, corn, cucumbers, fava beans, green beans, kohlrabi, lima beans, peas, peppers, summer squash, tomatoes, winter squash

Fruit: apricots, berries, cherries, figs, grapes, litchis, mangos, melons, nectarines, peaches, plums

AUGUST
Vegetables: avocados, beets, corn, cucumbers, fava beans, eggplant, green beans, kohlrabi, lima beans, peppers, summer squash, tomatoes, winter squash

Fruit: berries, cherries, figs, grapes, litchis, mangos, melons, nectarines, peaches, pears, plums

summer

SEPTEMBER
Vegetables: beets, beet greens, cauliflower, corn, eggplant, porcini mushrooms, summer squash, tomatoes, winter squash

Fruit: figs, grapes, melons, peaches, pears, plums

OCTOBER
Vegetables: beets, beet greens, cauliflower, collard greens, chanterelle mushrooms, lettuces, parsnips, summer squash, winter squash

Fruit: apples, coconuts, grapes, melons, peaches, pears, persimmons, pomegranates, tangerines

NOVEMBER
Vegetables: artichokes, beets, cabbage, cauliflower, celery, celery root, collard greens, chanterelle mushrooms, parsnips, rutabagas, winter squash, turnips

Fruit: apples, coconuts, dates, grapefruit, grapes, persimmons, pomegranates, tangerines

fall

Winter

December: Leeks and Beets

LEEKS

Leeks are a part of the onion family and are related to shallots, garlic, chives, and scallions. They have a sweet, delicate flavor all their own—much more flavorful than green onions. Leeks are available year-round in most regions. Like many vegetables, leeks contain a variety of antioxidants, vitamins, and minerals, particularly B vitamins and magnesium. Much like garlic, leeks have compounds that turn into allicin, a powerful antibacterial, antiviral, and antifungal substance. Allicin is also a big player in heart and liver health.

Leeks like well-drained soil and like to be in rows that have been built up a bit. The best place for growing leeks is in full sun with fertile, well-drained soil. When planting leeks in the garden, make a shallow trench about 4 to 5 inches deep and place the plants inside, spacing about 6 inches apart and covering with only a light amount of soil. Be sure to water leeks thoroughly and add a layer of organic mulch. I love to use mushroom compost.

As the leeks grow, use the excavated soil from the trench to slowly build up around the stem to keep out light. Be sure to harvest leeks before flowering occurs.

Leek tops should be dark green and firm, not limp or dried out. The bulb ends should have fringes of small, crisp-looking roots still attached; avoid split or soft bulbs, or those with large blemishes. It is essential to clean leeks well, as dirt, sand, and grit can collect between the layers. Refrigerate leeks up to one week, loosely wrapped in plastic or paper towel. Wait to trim the tops and roots until just before using.

> **Leeks grow best** in well-drained soil and like to be in rows that have been built up a bit. The best place for growing leeks is in full sun with fertile, well-drained soil.

Roasted Leeks

3 leeks, cleaned and dark green sections removed and then chopped

4 carrots, chopped

1 shallot or onion, chopped

2 tablespoons olive oil

2 tablespoons balsamic vinegar

salt and pepper to taste

Chop all vegetables and place on a baking sheet. Drizzle with olive oil, and sprinkle with salt and pepper. Roast at 350 degrees for about 20 minutes until tender and browned a bit. Drizzle with balsamic vinegar when done cooking. Serve immediately.

Baked Salmon with Leeks

1 big salmon filet or two small filets

3 cups leeks, cleaned and dark green sections removed and then sliced

½ cup grated parmesan cheese or nutritional yeast for dairy-free option

2 tablespoons olive oil

2 tablespoons lemon juice

1 teaspoon rosemary

1 teaspoon thyme

1 teaspoon rosemary (or one twig of fresh)

1 teaspoon sea salt

Lay salmon filet in an oven-safe dish then drizzle with olive oil and lemon juice all over. Sprinkle herbs, spices, and cheese or nutritional yeast on top. Spread leeks around salmon. Bake at 375 degrees for 30 to 40 minutes, or until salmon flakes apart when you touch it with a fork.

Leek and Potato Soup

4 to 5 leeks, cleaned and dark green sections removed

4 tablespoons cooked bacon for garnish

4 sweet potatoes, peeled and chopped

4 cloves garlic, minced

4 tablespoons chopped chives for garnish

6 cups chicken stock

2 cups coconut milk, raw milk, or heavy cream

1 teaspoon hot sauce

2 teaspoons Worcestershire sauce

1 tablespoon cooking fat

1 teaspoon dry mustard

1 teaspoon salt

1 teaspoon white pepper

Sauté garlic and leeks in cooking fat on medium heat in a large sauté pan (the most amazing smell ever). Cook until browned in some places (leeks should be soft and bright), about 8 minutes. Set aside.

Boil potatoes in chicken stock until they are soft enough to mash with a fork. Puree with an immersion or regular blender.

Add back in leeks and garlic, whisk dry mustard into cream/milk, and bring to a boil. Reduce heat and simmer for 3 to 5 minutes. Then add in hot sauce to taste, Worcestershire sauce, salt and pepper, and mix well. Garnish with chives and bacon.

This makes for a thick, hearty soup. If you want the soup to be a bit lighter, just add in more stock until it's the consistency you want.

Freeze in individual portions, in freezer bags, for a perfect easy lunch or dinner.

Side Tip:

If you don't have an immersion blender, BUY ONE! You can get one as cheap as $40 and they are such a time and stress saver!)

BEETS

Beets are extremely easy to grow and are *so* good for you. Roasted, slow cooked, raw, juiced, whatever. I flippin' *love* beets. They are packed with vitamins, nutrients, and antioxidants. Beets contain a compound called glycine betain, which lowers toxic metabolites in blood that lead to plaque formation in blood vessels. Along with that, nitrates in concentrated beet juice have also been found to lower blood pressure. Beets are another great source of B vitamins, as well as potassium and magnesium. The best part about beets? The whole plant can be eaten, and the leaves are just as packed with nutrients as the root, particularly vitamin C.

Direct seeding in the garden is the easiest way to grow beets. They can be grown in most types of soil but prefer that it be deep, well-drained, and include plenty of organic material, such as compost or aged manure. Too much nitrogen will cause beets to produce lots of greens, but little roots. Soak beet seeds in water for 24 hours before planting to aid germination. Beets prefer cool weather. For an early summer crop, sow seeds in a sunny spot, 3 to 4 weeks before your last frost. Plant seeds ½ inch deep, 2 inches apart if growing for greens, 3 to 4 inches apart if growing for the roots (but you can still harvest the greens, too). Sow seeds again in late summer for a fall crop. In frost-free areas, you can do a third planting in September for a winter harvest. Thin out the plants when they get a little bit bigger to give them more space. They can only grow as big as the room you give them, so if they have no room to grow, they will be tiny little radish-sized beets.

Harvest beet roots when they're 1½ to 3 inches in diameter for optimum flavor, tenderness, and texture. To remove the greens for cooking, hold the root in one hand and twist the tops off with the other hand, this minimizes "bleeding" and retains the moisture and flavor.

Beets are such a versatile and flavorful vegetable, they can be added to any meal. They hold up great in a slow cooker and are delicious roasted or fresh. They are actually quite sweet, so if you think you don't like beets, give them a try again. Fresh, in-season beets taste nothing like what comes from the can. Some people like to keep the skin on, cook them, and then peel them off afterwards, but I like to peel them like a carrot before I chop them for whatever meal I am cooking. Be warned your hands will turn bright pink, but it washes off in a couple of washes. Also, if you eat a lot of beets during one meal, the next time you go to the bathroom, it may look like blood. Don't freak out!

Beet Arugula Salad

4 beets, peeled and chopped

1 big bunch arugula

½ cup goat cheese

½ cup pecans or walnuts

1 tablespoon olive oil

1 tablespoon apple cider vinegar

Peel and chop the beets, put them on a cookie sheet, sprinkle salt, pepper, and olive oil, and roast in the oven at 350 degrees for about 25 minutes. Once they have cooled down a bit, add them to a bowl filled with arugula, cheese, and pecans. Add some more olive oil and apple cider vinegar. Toss and serve.

January: Citrus and Rhubarb

CITRUS

As most of you know, citrus fruits are packed with vitamin C—a powerful antioxidant that assists the immune system against infections. The acidity in these fruits comes from citric acid, which aids digestion and can even help clear kidney stones. Combined with a variety of other antioxidants, minerals, and fiber, citrus fruits are a powerhouse of health, something that has been recognized for centuries.

The Meyer lemon is about the only small citrus tree that is easy to grow unless you live in a tropical area. You can plant a Meyer lemon tree in a big pot and keep it on your porch and bring it indoors during the winter. Ask your local nursery if there are any frost-resistant varieties of citrus that do well in your area. If you are up north, you can get away with having a small citrus tree in a pot in your house as long as you keep the soil well drained and keep the tree in a sunny spot. Like most house plants, citrus prefer a sandy, slightly acidic, all-purpose mix. And get the largest pot you can afford and have room for so you don't have to repot every year.

When I used to think of citrus, only orange juice came to mind. But citrus can be used in many flavor combinations and citrus fruits like lemon and lime can be an immediate flavor booster or can be used to enhance many dishes. It's known for bringing out the other flavors of the dish. Try some of these flavor combinations some time to marinate meat or sauté vegetables: citrus, cranberry, and honey mustard; marmalade instead of BBQ on pork or chicken; or lime, soy sauce, and ginger.

Old School Marmalade

4 large Seville (bitter) oranges or any kind of oranges

8 large Cara Cara or navel oranges

2 large Meyer lemons

4½ cups sugar

Juice the oranges and lemons, putting any seeds and pith in a different bowl and set aside. Zest the lemons and set aside. Thinly peel the orange rinds with a vegetable peeler and cut into fine strips. Put all remaining skins, membranes, and seeds in a muslin towel or bag and tightly tie with twine. In a large heavy soup pot or dutch oven, combine citrus juices, zest, and rinds with the bagged skins and 4 cups water, bring to a boil, reduce heat, and simmer for 20 minutes. Remove from heat and remove bag to bowl. Add sugar to pot and stir well. Squeeze natural pectin from bag into pot, return to heat and bring to a fast boil. When mixture reaches 220 degrees, remove from heat, spoon into sterilized jars, and seal. Makes 6 cups.

Lemon-Ginger Salmon

2 4-ounce salmon filets

3 ounces white wine

2 tablespoons tamari sauce

2 tablespoons fresh ginger peeled and finely chopped

1 teaspoon pepper

1 tablespoon honey

juice of one lemon

Mix all ingredients (except salmon) in a bowl. Pour some of the liquid mixture on to the bottom of a casserole dish, put salmon in dish, then add more mixture on top. Broil in oven for 3 to 5 minutes. Flip salmon over and broil for another 3 to 5 minutes. Serve immediately, with a few squirts of fresh lemon juice to garnish.

RHUBARB

Rhubarbs are known mostly for being in baked goods, but they are also great in a salad with goat cheese. I have memories of my grandma's rhubarb crisp. It was heavenly. I loved how happy it made my father when she made it for family dinners at her house, and I remember thinking she made it especially for him and I wondered how that would feel if someone ever made me something simply because it was my favorite. Throughout my childhood, I observed with shock and amazement my friends' mothers who would cook things just because those were their kids' favorite things to eat. That was the entire reason I learned how to cook. I was determined to be able to express love in this way for my future family and give them what I never got.

Very rich in B vitamins, red rhubarb, in particular, is a delicious source of health. While you can get green varieties, the red stalks have higher beta carotene content and vitamin K1. Watch out for oxalic acid in this vegetable; it binds to the naturally occurring minerals and makes them nearly impossible to absorb. The good news is that oxalic acid can be broken down by cooking or fermenting the vegetable, which frees up calcium, iron, and potassium to be absorbed during digestion. However, eating too much can have a laxative effect.

Rhubarb is a hardy cool-weather plant, so it does well in northern states and during the winter in more southern states. It is not susceptible to many diseases or pests. Rhubarb may grow in less-than-ideal soil conditions, but does best in a moist, well-drained garden that contains plenty of organic matter and that has a pH level of 6.0 to 6.8. Dig holes approximately 10 inches deep and plant your rhubarb shoots with the crown buds 2 inches below the surface of the soil. Space crowns 2 to 4 feet apart, in rows 3 to 4 feet apart. You can place them a bit closer in a smaller garden. Don't cut the stalks the first year, and pick lightly the second year to give the plant time to establish its roots. After the third year, you may harvest the entire plant. Perennial rhubarb will grow for four or five years before it will need to be divided. Mulch around your rhubarb plants in the late fall or early winter to protect the roots from frigid weather, but don't cover the crowns or they may rot. After the first hard frost, cut down any stalks that are still standing, and throw them on your compost pile. The leaves are mildly poisonous but the toxins will break down quickly and won't harm your compost.

If you are buying rhubarb at the farmers' market or grocery store, look for thin, red, crisp stalks, as those have the best texture. If stalks are floppy, it indicates they were picked too long ago. When you get home, wrap them in plastic or paper towel and refrigerate for up to one week.

Red Rhubarb is particularly rich in B vitamins, beta carotene, and vitamin K1.

Grain-Free Rhubarb Crisp

4-5 cups rhubarb, chopped (about 5 stalks)

5-6 cups organic strawberries (halved or quartered, depending on size)

1½ teaspoons orange zest

¼ cup honey

1 teaspoon vanilla

For the Crumble Top:

4 cups almond meal

1½ cups finely chopped pecans

3 teaspoons cinnamon

3 teaspoons vanilla

2/3 cup butter or coconut oil

¼ cup maple syrup

Combine the first five ingredients in a large bowl and mix well. Grease a 9 x 13 inch pan and preheat your oven to 350 degrees. Pour fruit mixture into greased pan.

Combine dry ingredients for crumble topping, mixing well, and stir to combine. Using your hands, crumble the topping over the fruit and place in the oven on lowest rack so the top doesn't burn. Bake for about 35 minutes or until the fruit is bubbly and the top is nicely browned and crisp.

Rhubarb Chutney

1 medium onion, finely chopped

1 pound rhubarb, cut into ½-inch pieces

½ cup raisins

1 tablespoon ginger, peeled and minced

½ cup honey

2 tablespoons olive oil

1 cinnamon stick

1 tablespoon sherry vinegar

In a saucepan, heat oil on medium heat. Add onion and cook until softened, 5 to 6 minutes. Add rhubarb, raisins, honey, ginger, and cinnamon stick. Cook over medium, stirring occasionally, until rhubarb begins to break down, 6 to 8 minutes. Remove cinnamon stick and stir in vinegar. Serve with ham or pork. It can keep in the fridge in an unopened canning jar for several months; once you open it, use it within a couple of weeks.

February: Greens and Brussels Sprouts

GREENS

I love my winter garden because it is so easy. Bugs and disease are less common in a winter garden, and I always have copious amounts of greens for fresh salads. Penelope loves to come out into the garden and harvest with me. Greens are one of those vegetables that you can start harvesting sooner, so it is a great plant option to start with for impatient kids or adults. Greens are really easy to plant directly as seeds or to transfer small baby plants. Either way, give them plenty of space on all sides; greens can grow pretty wide and they need room for their leaves to grow.

Kale will produce and produce and produce. When you are harvesting leaves from your kale plant, take from the bottom; this way your plant will keep growing and producing well. Wash leaves well, as they are so close to the ground and often have a lot of dirt on them. They are the best tasting after a frost, so that is a great time for a harvest. Be sure to always remove stems before cooking with them; they are too tough and don't taste good. Kale holds up well in a slow cooker, so you could add some fresh kale to many slow cooker recipes to get more greens into your diet.

There are plenty of cold hardy plants you can grow during moderate winters, like Brussels sprouts, spinach, arugula, kale, and a wide variety of lettuces. They are all very easy to grow, especially kale. Even in the places with the coldest winters, you can have indoor windowsill herb plants to give you some fresh greens. Pretty much any herb will taste great with olive oil to make a pesto. Or throw some in your salad for lots of flavor. Really, just throw fresh herbs into anything you are cooking, you really can't go wrong so don't be afraid of messing up.

Leafy greens, like kale and spinach, are versatile plants that can beef up the nutrition content for a variety of foods. These greens are very rich in beta carotene, vitamin C, B vitamins, and a variety of minerals (particularly iron). Much like rhubarb, some leafy greens, like spinach, contain oxalic acid and must be cooked in order to get the maximum benefit. While eating too much can actually pose a problem, moderate amounts contribute greatly to fighting cancer.

To prepare collard greens or kale as a side dish, the traditional method is cooking them in pork and simmering them for a long time. The vitamins in these greens are fat-soluble, meaning you need to cook them and eat with animal fat to absorb the vitamins. Simmering them a long time helps the greens to retain their vitamins (high heat can destroy some vitamins), but it also helps breakdown the bitterness and give them great flavor.

Kale Chips

1 head kale, washed and thoroughly dried

2 tablespoons olive oil

1 teaspoon sea salt

1 teaspoon cayenne pepper

Remove the ribs from the kale and cut into 1 ½-inch pieces. Put in a big bowl, drizzle with olive oil, add spices, and toss. Lay seasoned kale on a baking sheet and bake about 20 minutes at 250 degress until crisp, turning the leaves halfway through. Chips will store for about a week in an airtight container in the fridge.

Creamed Spinach

3 10-ounce bunches of spinach, well washed and stemmed

3 garlic cloves, minced

1 teaspoon sea salt

½ teaspoon of nutmeg

1 teaspoon pepper

1 cup chicken stock

1 cup water

¾ cup heavy cream or coconut milk

4 tablespoons butter

3 tablespoons arrowroot powder

Bring water to a boil in a large saucepan over high heat and salt lightly. In batches, add in spinach, stirring until each batch is wilted before adding the next. Cover tightly, reduce heat to medium and cook about 5 minutes until spinach is tender. Using a colander, drain spinach over a large bowl to keep the water. Measure out 1¼ cups of the leftover spinach water and pour into a separate bowl; add in broth and cream and mix together. Rinse spinach in cold water, squeeze to remove excess water, and chop. Heat butter and garlic in a skillet over medium heat. Add in flour and whisk together for about 2 minutes, then add the broth/water/cream mixture. Cook about 5 minutes, whisking often until thickened. Stir in spinach and add in salt, pepper and nutmeg. Mix all together and serve immediately.

Spinach Pie

½ pound of bacon

3 hard-boiled eggs, chopped

2 uncooked eggs

5 10-ounce bunches spinach, washed well

1 onion, chopped

¼ teaspoon freshly grated nutmeg

Almond flour pie crust (on page 35)

Boil the spinach for 10 to 15 minutes and place in a colander. When the spinach is cool, use your hands and press all the water out. Chop and set aside.

In a pan, cook the bacon and set aside. Next, sauté the onions in the bacon grease. When the onions are done, take the pan off the stove. Add the spinach, bacon, and hard-boiled eggs. Add most of two beaten large eggs (save a little bit for later), pepper, and nutmeg into the pan and toss with the onion mixture. Pour the spinach mixture into a pie pan lined with crust and cover with another pie crust. Poke a few holes with a fork and brush the top of the pie with the leftover beaten egg. Bake for 30 minutes at 350 degrees or until it's a nice light-brown color. Actually, you can bake it right away, freeze it as-is to bake later, or bake it and then freeze it.

Spinach pie is such a *bitch* to make. Or, rather, it is a labor of love. It is an amazing tasting comfort food. It's also worth the time and effort if your child, or your man-child, won't eat vegetables. You are getting about five servings of vegetables in every slice!!!

To make this recipe a little easier, divide the work into two batches. First, boil the eggs and spinach, chop the onions, and make the almond flour crust (press half the crust into the pie pan and then leave the other half for the top crust rolled in a ball in the middle, and cover with Saran wrap in the fridge). The next block of time should be within 48 hours to finish this meal. During the second half of the process, you would cook the bacon, sauté the onions, combine spices and spinach together, and then roll out the top of the crust.

BRUSSELS SPROUTS

Most people have never really had good Brussels sprouts. They believe they dislike them because, too often, they have been served soggy, overcooked, and bitter sprouts. Home-grown Brussels sprouts, however, are a whole other experience and you will love the sweet, nutty taste fresh sprouts have. Sprouts are better the fresher they are, but will keep in the fridge for a couple of weeks. Even store-bought Brussels sprouts are delicious when you use my roasting recipe—*I promise*!

Surprisingly, Brussels sprouts are not only an incredible source for antioxidants, but also have antibacterial and antiviral properties. Combined with vitamin C, beta carotene, B vitamins, and several important minerals, Brussels sprouts are an especially powerful tool against various cancers and other diseases. High in vitamin K1, it is possible to eat too much and thicken the blood. As another oxalate food, make sure you cook them thoroughly!

Brussels sprouts grow best in full sun. To avoid disease and pest problems, allow three years between plantings of the cabbage-family (cabbage, kale, cauliflower, and broccoli) in the same area. Brussels sprouts grow really well in soil that was previously planted with legumes, like peas and beans, grow well in either flat rows or raised beds. It is very important that the soil is rich and well prepared because sprouts have such a long growing season.

Plant 18 to 24 inches apart with 2 to 3 feet between rows, and keep weeded or use mulch to hinder weed development. Pinch off top leaves to encourage side growth. Give Brussels sprouts steady moisture, especially when the air temperatures rise over 80 degrees because hot, dry spells will stunt sprout formation. Mulching will help keep soil temperatures cool and moisture levels steady, while helping keep weeds under control. As sprouts form in the corner of where the leaf grows from the main stalk, snap off the leaves beneath them. This will help channel the plant's energy into forming the sprouts and will make it easier to actually harvest the sprouts once they are full size.

Three to four weeks before harvesting, when the sprouts are ½ to ¾ inch in diameter, you can do one of two things: If you want the sprouts to ripen all at once, pinch off the growing point (the cluster of leaves at the very top of the main stem) to help the plant concentrate on sprout formation. Or you can allow the plant to grow naturally and your sprouts will mature over a longer period of time, extending your harvest; this is what I like to do so that on any given evening I can go out with my daughter and pick some for dinner to be quickly roasted up for a side dish.

Slow Cooker Brussels Sprouts

1 pound Brussels sprouts

3 tablespoons cooking fat

1 tablespoon dijon mustard

1 teaspoon sea salt

1 teaspoon black pepper

½ cup water

Wash and trim the ends off of each Brussels sprout and cut in half. Toss into a 2-quart slow cooker. Add butter, mustard, salt, pepper, and water. Cover and cook on low for 4 to 5 hours, or on high for 2 to 3 hours. Stir well to distribute the sauce before serving. The sprouts on the outer edge get brown and bit crispy.

Roasted Brussel Sprouts

1 pound Brussels sprouts, trimmed and halved lengthwise

2 tablespoons extra-virgin olive oil

1 teaspoon sea salt

1 teaspoon ground black pepper

1 lemon juiced

Preheat oven to 400 degrees. In a bowl, toss Brussels sprouts with oil, salt and pepper, and then spread out on a rimmed baking sheet and roast, stirring once or twice, until deep golden brown, crisp outside and tender inside, about 30 to 35 minutes. The leaves that are loose will be especially brown and crispy. Transfer to a bowl and serve. You could add variation to this veggie dish by adding cranberries and walnuts one day or rosemary and parmesan another time.

Spring

March: Radishes, Carrots, and Peas

RADISHES

Radishes were the first vegetable I ever grew, when I was 10 years old. I remember being so shocked when they turned out to be a REAL vegetable! I just could not believe that an actual vegetable grew from a tiny seed, but I was hooked. That year, I also grew sunflowers and became so obsessed with sunflowers that I even painted them all over my bedroom walls. (Better than radishes, right?)

Radishes are one of the few root vegetables that are low in calories. Both fresh and cooked radishes have been shown to help with cancer prevention. While they are high in vitamin C, they have moderate to low levels of B vitamins and minerals, but are higher in folic acid and potassium.

Both radish and carrots are easily grown in deep containers if you don't have a garden. Rake the area to create big clumps of soil and dig tiny holes about 1 inch deep. I just push my finger into the ground to the first line of wrinkles on my hand and call it an inch, but you could get a special tool that will help you measure the proper depth. One seed per hole, each hole about 2 inches apart.

You should see the first shoots appear after a couple of weeks, but allow them to grow for another week before thinning out to 1 seedling per inch. If your radish is not properly thinned at this time, then you will have problems with your radish forming to a good size. During this time, you will also need to keep an eye on weeds, as radish plants do not compete well for nutrients.

Make sure that they get a reasonable and regular supply of water, otherwise the bulbs can crack if they are left to mature too long. You should be looking to harvest your radishes as soon as they are ready, usually around 5 weeks after sowing. If you leave them too long, they can lose their crispness and become far too bitter to eat.

Radishes are great cooked, and they taste amazing simply sautéed with salt and butter. They are also delicious raw, sliced and eaten with cheese, or with a dip instead of a cracker.

After you do your shopping, if you know you're not going to be able to get to your radishes right away, trim them of their greens and put them in a jar. Put enough water in the jar to cover the radishes and store it in the fridge. They'll keep for a good 4 to 5 days this way without losing any of their crunch or flavor.

Roasted Radish

16 ounces radishes, chopped

3 tablespoons olive oil

2 teaspoons salt

Wash, trim, and quarter radishes. Toss radishes in small bowl with olive oil. Spread on cookie sheet or roasting pan and sprinkle with salt. Roast at 375 degrees for 20 to 25 minutes. You'll know they're done when you see the color deepen a bit and the radishes will appear a bit wrinkly.

Radish Dip

1 bunch radishes

a few basil leaves

8 ounces cream cheese

salt and pepper to taste

Puree all ingredients in food processor. Note: Radishes have lots of water in them, so the more radishes you use, the more watery the dip will be.

Radish-Mushroom Chicken Soup

2 pounds chicken thighs

8 ounces sugar snap or snow peas

2 cups sliced radishes

2 pounds mushrooms

1 onion, chopped

6 cloves garlic, minced

1 teaspoon dried thyme

salt and pepper to taste

4 cups chicken stock

½ cup dry white wine

1 tablespoon apple cider vinegar

In a deep pot, sauté onion, garlic, and mushrooms in butter about 5 minutes. Add chicken stock, wine, chicken, veggies, spices, and apple cider vinegar, and bring to a boil. While the soup is coming to a boil, scrape the bottom of the pot to loosen all the browned bits of onion and garlic. Reduce heat and simmer for about 2 hours.

Can't get to your radishes right away?

Trim them of their greens and put them in a jar. Put enough water in the jar to cover the radishes and store it in the fridge. They'll keep for a good four to five days this way without losing any of their crunch or flavor.

PEAS

Green peas are especially high in folate (folic acid), which is a very important nutrient for pregnant women. Legumes like peas are high in plant sterols, which help maintain healthy cholesterol levels in the body. With plenty of other B vitamins and iron, across the board, peas are one of the most nutritious members of the legume family. However, peas are high in starch and plant sugars, and should be consumed in moderation.

Sow seeds outdoors 4 to 6 weeks before last spring frost, when soil temperatures reach 45 degrees. Peas are best grown in temperatures below 70 degrees, so they are the perfect easy spring vegetable for lots of places. I always sow the seeds directly outside after the last danger of frost. Plant the seeds 1 inch deep and about 6 inches apart. This is a vegetable you can plant close together because the only place they are going is up. You will want to get some stakes and twine and tie them up as they grow.

Keep your peas well picked to encourage more pods to develop. This makes for another great daily afternoon garden visit with your child for an easy dinner side.

Always use two hands when you pick peas. Secure the vine with one hand and pull the peas off with your other hand. They are easy to grow, but have a very limited growing season. If you missed your peas' peak period, you can still pick, dry, and shell them for use in winter soups. Also, peas do not stay fresh long after harvest, so enjoy them while you can! Peas can be frozen or kept in the refrigerator for about 5 days. Place in paper bags, then wrap in plastic.

Peas go great with everything. Add raw peas to salads. Sauté them with butter and salt for a simple side dish. If you have a bounty of them, add them to any slow cooker meal the last 30 minutes of cooking for an added green vegetable.

Split Pea Soup

2 packs bacon

4 cups peas (fresh or frozen)

3 cups mirepoix (even mixture of carrot, onion, and celery)

½ teaspoon red chili pepper flakes (more or less, to taste)

2 bay leaves

1 teaspoon dried parsley.

4 cups chicken stock

Because of the bacon, this soup comes out like a poopy green color, but I don't give a crap (pun intended!)—it tastes amazing! And remember bacon (good quality, grass fed, and nitrate free) is good for you!

Cook your bacon in a 4- or 5-quart pan, remov, and set aside. Sauté mirepoix for 10 to 15 minutes, until soft. Add in corn, peas, stock, and spices, and bring to a boil for a few minutes before turning the heat down. Use an immersion blender and blend to a soup consistency. Add more stock if you want a thinner soup, less if you want it thicker. Simmer on low for about an hour. Freeze leftovers in individual sandwich freezer bags.

Carrot, Pea, and Radish Salad

1 pound peas, cleaned and trimmed

2 carrots, peeled and shredded

5 radishes, thinly sliced

2 tablespoons fig vinegar

1 tablespoon olive oil

salt and pepper to taste

Toss vegetables together in a bowl. In a separate bowl, whisk together vinegar and oil. Toss in with vegetables, stir to incorporate. Season to taste.

CARROTS

Carrots are so fun to grow with kids. Seeing the excitement of them pulling up on one of the tops and discovering a beautiful carrot is just plain awesome.

Carrots are best known for beta carotene, a precursor for vitamin A production, which creates the rich purple, red, yellow, brown, and orange colors for this root vegetable. Traditional medicine followers have used carrots to increase blood to the pelvic region, as well as to ease digestive problems. Being especially rich in B vitamins, carrots are a great source of folic acid for pregnant women.

In the spring, sow carrot seeds in fertile, well-worked soil about two weeks before your last frost date. In cool climates, continue planting every three weeks until midsummer. In summer, begin sowing seeds for fall and winter carrots 10 to 12 weeks before your average first fall frost.

Carrots take about 14 to 28 days to germinate, so be patient and keep your seeds moist during that time! Thin carrots so they are 1 inch apart from each other when their greens are 3 to 5 inches tall. If they don't have enough space, you will grow a thin, little carrot.

Pull or dig spring-sown carrots when roots reach mature size and show rich color. Taste improves as carrots mature, but do not leave mature carrots in warm soil any longer than necessary (many critters like carrots). Summer-sown carrots that mature in cool fall soil can be left in the ground longer, but should be dug before the ground freezes to preserve their quality.

Remove tops to prevent moisture loss, rinse clean, and store in a refrigerator or cold root cellar. Most varieties keep for several months in the fridge. Carrots also may be canned, pickled, dried, or frozen. If I ever have carrots that are getting soggy but are not ready to be thrown out, I juice them or put them in a smoothie so not to go to waste.

Braised Sweet Carrots

1 pound carrots, peeled and chopped (approximately 3 cups)

1-2 cups chicken stock (just enough to cover the carrots)

2 tablespoons honey

Place carrots in a pot with stock and honey and cook on medium-high heat. Cook until stock is gone and carrots are soft, about 30 to 40 minutes.

Soggy carrots? Not-so-crisp carrots are perfect for juicing or are great additions to smoothies.

April: Strawberries and Chard

STRAWBERRIES

I am not even going to lie . . . strawberries are a bitch to grow. They require very particular soil, moisture, and sun amounts. Birds, bugs, and pests love them. And unless you fertilize them generously, they don't produce well. I honestly do not understand how commercial organic strawberry growers do it. I have tried several different methods and several different places in my garden and the best thing that works for me is planting them in big containers on the porch, where they are a bit more protected. Growing them this way means I only get a one to three strawberries a day, but it is a fun thing to do with my daughter to check if there are any ripe strawberries ready. She always exclaims loudly, "Mama, I found one!!!" Her joy and exuberance fill me with such joy and one of the things I love most about gardening with her.

I have an ongoing love affair with strawberries. I grew up in a rural farming community in South Florida, where many of the farmers grow strawberries. I have many memories picking my own strawberries and getting a strawberry milkshake at the local farm stand. Last year, I got to introduce Penelope to a strawberry milkshake from that same farm stand and it was such a thrill to see her little face light up when she took her first sip. When I was younger, my Godmother lived in Plant City and I used to love going to the Strawberry Festival in the spring. My Godmother was an avid gardener and artist. She had the most amazing rose garden. I loved going to her house and seeing everything in its place and perfectly clean and her perfect garden. She had a gorgeous sunroom and she would pick some roses from her garden and then paint a still life painting. As most of you know from reading my blog and books, my childhood was far from perfect and filled with abuse and neglect, but I was so blessed to have many influential women in my life and I was lucky to be a child that was so observant and had a good memory! As a kid, I would just observe everything and tuck my observations away to pull out later when I was older and could do things differently in my own home and for my own family.

In Florida, you can get local strawberries from December to May, but the peak is around April. Strawberries in season by themselves are an explosion of flavor in your mouth. Or, like my great-grandmother in Kansas used to do when the strawberries were not in peak season, you can put strawberries in a bowl and sprinkle sugar all over them, then let them sit awhile and have the sugar soak in to sweeten them up.

Strawberries are more powerful than given credit for. Much higher in vitamin C than oranges, strawberries are actually in the top 20 fruits for antioxidant levels. This means they're not only a potent ally in the fight against cancer, but also help with aging, inflammation, and even neurological function.

Fresca Con Creama

When I first went to Argentina to meet my husband's family, before we were married, we also went down south to Patagonia. We went to a local restaurant and snarfed down a beef stew, similar to the recipe in my first cookbook, and had strawberries and cream for dessert, and it was strawberry season. We had learned our lesson the first night when we waited to order dessert after our meal, and they were gone, so the second night, we sat down and ordered our *fruitillas y crema* along with our meal, because we were not missing out again.

1 pound strawberries

1 cup heavy whipping cream, the best you can buy or make your own.

1 tablespoons of maple syrup or sugar

1 teaspoon vanilla extract

Whip cream, syrup or sugar, and vanilla lightly in a bowl. Cream will thicken up as it's whipped. Add some freshly washed strawberries, greens removed and cut in half, on top of the cream and . . . welcome to Heaven.

CHARD

Swiss chard is so fun to grow, especially if you plant the rainbow varieties. You can talk about colors with your children as they are out in the garden and have a more unique experience to teach them colors.

Chard is particularly high in vitamin C, vitamin K1, and folate. While chard also has a rich array of minerals, it also contains oxalic acid that prevents them from being absorbed. Simply cooking down the chard will break up the acid and allow the necessary minerals, such as iron, be absorbed by the intestines.

In spring, sow directly in the garden two weeks after your last frost date, or start seeds indoors three to four weeks before your last frost date and set seedlings out just as the last frost passes. In fall, start seeds about 10 weeks before your first frost date, and set the seedlings out when they are four weeks old. Plant seeds ½ inch deep and 3 inches apart. Set out seedlings 12 inches apart.

You can add fresh chard to any soup or stew. You can also add finely shredded chard to any slaw or salad. As with most vegetables, if you think you don't like them, roast or sauté them with lots of good grass-fed butter and sea salt and you are sure to like them.

Sautéed Chard

1 pound chard, chopped

3 garlic cloves, chopped

½ cup almond, pecans, or walnuts

1 teaspoon thyme

1 teaspoon sea salt

2 tablespoons cooking fat

Add oil to pan, and add in the rest of the ingredients and sauté over medium-high heat. Chard is done when it is soft and slightly browned.

Slow Cooker Swiss Chard "Lasagna"

2 28-ounce jars diced tomatoes, drained, or 8 fresh tomatoes, chopped

1 bunch Swiss chard, stems chopped and leaves torn into large pieces

1 to 2 eggplants or 3 to 4 zucchini, thinly sliced the long way to act as "lasagna noodles"

3 garlic cloves, chopped

2 tablespoons oregano

2 tablespoons parsley

2 teaspoons salt

2 teaspoons pepper

16 ounces ricotta (or cashew spread for dairy free)

½ cup parmesan cheese, grated (or nutritional yeast for dairy free)

12 ounces mozzarella, grated

In a medium bowl, combine the tomatoes, garlic, oregano, 1 teaspoon salt, and 1 teaspoon pepper. In another medium bowl, combine the ricotta, parsley, parmesan, and 1 teaspoon salt and pepper. Spoon ⅓ cup of the tomato mixture into the ceramic insert of a slow cooker. Top with a single layer of the thinly sliced vegetable "noodles," breaking them to fit as necessary. Add half the Swiss chard. Dollop with a third of the ricotta mixture and a third of the remaining tomato mixture. Sprinkle with a third of the mozzarella. Add another layer of noodles and repeat with the other ingredients. Finish with a layer of noodles and the remaining ricotta mixture, tomato mixture, and mozzarella. Set the slow cooker to low and cook, covered, about 2 hours.

Handwritten notes:

⅓ Tom mix / Zuch / ½ Chard / ⅓ Ricotta / ⅓ Tom

⅓ Mozz / Zuch / ½ Chard / ⅓ Ricotta / ⅓ Tom / ⅓ Mozz

Zuch / Ricotta / Tom / Mozz / Parm?

May: Mushrooms and Mangoes

MUSHROOMS

Mushrooms are a very interesting food. Made up primarily of water, mushrooms have very few calories or carbohydrates, no sodium, and are one of the only plant foods to contain no vitamin C. More interestingly, when placed under UV lights, mushrooms can actually begin producing vitamin D2, something that is only found in animals. Under normal conditions, mushrooms frequently contain significant levels of potassium, copper, selenium, and B vitamins.

I have never grown mushrooms before, but this year, I noticed a couple of mushroom-growing kits at my local natural foods grocery store that I want to try. It looks really simple and like something that would be fun to do with kids.

Or, you can go the DIY route and grow mushrooms on oak tree logs. First you get some oak tree logs, drill holes into the logs, insert the spores (you can buy them online), then cover the holes with wax. (Mushrooms do not need chlorophyll to grow.) Water them every couple of weeks if the weather is dry. Then you wait for them to do their thing. It can take from six months to two years for them to grow, so be patient!

A fancy cook will tell you to brush each mushroom clean because you don't want to get a mushroom wet. If you are a fancy cook, you can do that. If you are a lazy cook like me and think good enough is just fine, then dunk the mushroom in a bowl of cold water and agitate the water with your hand for a few seconds. Drain the water and pat the mushrooms dry on a towel.

Mushroom Onion Chicken Soup

2 pounds chicken thighs

8 garlic cloves, minced

3 lemons

3 cups white mushrooms, sliced

2 cups onion, chopped

2 cups asparagus, cut into bite size pieces

2 teaspoons salt

2 teaspoons ground black pepper

1 teaspoon chili powder

1 tablespoon dried rosemary

8 cups chicken broth

¼ cup sesame seeds, toasted

Combine all ingredients (except chicken broth) into two separate gallon-sized freezer bags. Lay flat and place in freezer.

On the day of cooking, place contents of bags into your slow cooker and add chicken broth. Cook on low for 8 hours or on high for 4 hours. Serve sprinkled with a teaspoon or two of toasted sesame seeds.

Mushroom Grilled Cheese Sandwich

2 Portobello mushrooms, stems and gills removed

2 tablespoons of cooking fat

sea salt and pepper

4 slices of sprouted whole-grain sandwich bread or 4 slices of eggplant (or, Against All Grain has a good grain-free bread recipe that I like)

4 tablespoons of pesto

4 ounces of Gruyere cheese

To remove the gills from the mushrooms, flip the mushroom upside down so you can see the gills (ribbon like ridges on the underside), and gently scrape out with a spoon.

Heat butter in a skillet and add mushrooms, flat side down, and cook until seared on the bottom, about 4 minutes. Turn mushrooms and cook another 2 minutes, until tender. Transfer mushroom to a plate and set aside. Add more fat and add two slices of bread or eggplant, having spread pesto on one slice (make sure pesto is up and not touching the skillet) put mushroom cap on slice of bread with pesto. Add cheese to other slice of bread or eggplant slice. When cheese has started to melt, put cheese slice of bread on top of pesto/mushroom slice of bread and gently press together. I usually use another cast-iron skillet on top of the sandwich while it is cooking to press it down, but you could also use a fancy panini press. Cook until bread is golden brown, about 5 minutes.

MANGOES

Most of the mango varieties you find in the supermarket are not very tasty. The best mangoes never make it to a grocery store, as they have a really short "shelf life" and bruise very easily. Mangoes are hard to ship and store. I had access to them when I lived in South Florida as a little girl. And then even in North Florida, one my local farmers would drive up tons of mangoes from an organic farm in South Florida and sell them at the farmers' market during the summer. And now that we live in South Florida again, I am already dreaming of the day that we can buy our own house and have a little grove of our own. My husband has already planted two small mangos from seed to start experimenting.

The avocado grove I grew up on also had mango trees and pretty much everyone I knew, family and friends, had a mango tree in their yard. My Granny used to make the best mango cobbler from a tree in her yard. My friend's mom made the best chutney. I remember going to their house as a kid and seeing her kitchen filled to the brim with mangos as she was boiling and canning the chutney. At first glance, it looked like mangoes filled every counter, container, and shelf.

The nutritional content for mangoes varies widely across the different varieties. However, most mangoes with orange-yellow colors will contain significant amounts of carotenoids, such as beta-carotene, which are precursors for vitamin A production. Generally, they are also a good source of potassium, vitamin C, vitamin E, and vitamin B6. As with most fruits, mangoes have a variety of antioxidants and have shown some promise for fighting cancers.

Mango trees do not fruit every year, tending to alternate years based on the weather, which means it's not every year that your kitchen will be taken over with mangoes. And like other flowering/fruiting trees, it takes a long time to establish roots and for the tree to have the strength and stamina to really produce. Blooming is strongly affected by weather; dryness stimulates flowering and rainy weather discourages it. Temperature is very important with mango trees. Cold weather is a major health factor; they die or suffer great damage at 32 degrees. In Southern Florida, mango trees begin to bloom in late November and continue until February or March, inasmuch as there are early, medium, and late varieties.

Mango Salsa

- 2 cups diced mango
- ½ cup diced green onion
- 1 tablespoon diced red jalapeno
- 3 tablespoons fresh lime juice
- 1 tablespoon honey

Chop all ingredients and mix in a bowl. Perfect with tacos.

Mangoes contain carotenoids, such as beta-carotene, and are a good source of potassium, vitamin C, vitamin E, and vitamin B6.

No whey? Don't use whey powder. Instead, substitute 3 teaspoons of sea salt.

Mango Chutney

3 cups ripe mango, peeled and cubed

1 tablespoon ginger, peeled and minced

2 red peppers, seeded and cut into small pieces

1 small onion, chopped

1 jalapeno pepper, seeded and chopped

½ cup fresh mint leaves, chopped

½ cup cilantro, chopped

2 tablespoons honey

½ cup fresh lemon or lime juice

½ cup filtered water

Either 2 teaspoons sea salt + ¼ cup liquid whey OR 3 teaspoons salt and no whey

Cube the mango and give it a good squish with a potato masher. Don't pulverize it completely, just go about halfway there.

In a large glass bowl, add chopped peppers, mint, coriander, grated ginger, honey, lemon, and onion. Mix just a little with an immersion blender, or pound it with a meat tenderizer/mortar and pestle. Add the mango mush to the other ingredients and mix. Add 2 teaspoons sea salt, ¼ cup of liquid whey, and ½ cup of water. If you don't have liquid whey, do not use whey powder. Simply skip the whey and use 3 teaspoons of salt instead.

Mix well, and transfer to a pickling jar, leaving some space at the top of the jar. Let it sit on the counter for about two days, and then transfer to the refrigerator. Use within two months, or freeze in small portions. Tastes great with chicken or fish.

Summer

June: Zucchini/Squash, Blueberries, and Tomatoes

ZUCCHINI/SQUASH

Squash is not really a vegetable but a fruit from a vine. It is probably the most versatile hot-weather produce; it can be grilled, sautéed, stuffed, and roasted, served raw in salads, simmered in soups, and even used in batter for baked goods.

Although low in antioxidant power, zucchini makes up for it by being one of the lowest calorie vegetables. Among the positive aspects of zucchini, it contains higher levels of folate, potassium, and vitamin C.

Have you ever heard stories of people dropping off bags of zucchini or squash on porches and running away in the summer? If you are growing zucchini or squash, you will soon see they are impressive producers and understand the stories of being "squash bombed." It is hard to use up all your zucchini that you produce, so don't get overzealous and plant a ton of plants the first time you try to plant zucchini, just do three at first and go from there. Zucchini is a part of the summer squash family that also includes crookneck squash and pattypan squash.

As squash are prolific growers, give them plenty of room in your garden. Picking the flowers and frying them is a good way to control the size of the crop. Summer squash is grown very easily from seed. You can either start seeds indoors, three to four weeks before your last frost date, or sow them directly in the garden after all danger of frost has passed. Plant seeds in hills of six seeds, and thin to the three strongest seedlings after they have their first true leaves. Summer squash should be planted in full sun, in rich, well-drained soil that has been amended with compost and manure—these plants are heavy feeders!

Harvest when zucchini is on the small side; you don't want to let them grow huge or you will lose flavor. Give squash a light scrub wash to get rid of any dirt and clinging grit.

Grain-Free Mac & Cheese with Zucchini "Pasta"

I made this meal for the first time at a baby shower I hosted. I did half with zucchini and half with gluten-free elbow pasta. And people at the shower actually liked the grain-free better!

If you want it grain free: 10 shredded zucchini (about 5 cups)

If you just want it gluten free: 16 ounces, al dente cooked gluten-free macaroni noodles

7 tablespoons cooking fat

4 tablespoons arrowroot flour

2 cups milk

1 teaspoon salt

¼ teaspoon fresh ground pepper, or to taste

½ teaspoon garlic powder

½ teaspoon onion powder

¼ teaspoon cayenne

8 ounces cheddar cheese (about 2 cups)

4 ounces gruyere (about 1 cup)

4 ounces provolone (about 1 cup)

5 ounces parmesan cheese (about 1 cup) (*I used a French mimolette, which is similar to parmesan in flavor but a fancy-pants version, and then sprinkled regular parmesan on top. Regular parmesan throughout works just the same.)

2 teaspoons hot sauce (optional)

Preheat oven to 350 degrees. Put 2 tablespoons of unsalted butter in a 3-quart baking dish. Set aside.

Fill a large pot half full with water. Cover and bring water to boil over high heat. Boil zucchini for just a few minutes, until they are bright green. If doing gluten-free pasta, add gluten-free macaroni (elbow) noodles and a pinch of salt and return water to a boil. Cook according to package directions, until al dente (beginning to soften but still somewhat firm to the bite).

While pasta is cooking, shred cheeses and make the cheese sauce. Melt 4 tablespoons of butter in a medium saucepan over low heat. Whisk in 4 tablespoons of arrowroot and cook for 2 minutes, whisking constantly. Slowly whisk in milk, increase heat to medium and whisk until mixture thickens.

Remove from heat. Add salt, pepper, garlic powder, onion powder, cayenne (optional), hot sauce (optional), 1 cup shredded cheddar cheese, ½ cup Parmesan and all of the Swiss and Fontina cheese. Stir until cheeses melt and mixture is smooth and creamy. Put the baking dish with butter in the preheated oven and leave just until butter melts. Remove and coat bottom and sides of the dish with butter using a pastry brush.

Drain, rinse, and pat dry cooked pasta. Pour half of the pasta in the baking dish and cover with about half of the cheese sauce. Distribute remaining pasta on top and evenly cover with remaining cheese sauce. Lightly salt and pepper and bake for 45 minutes or until top is golden and bubbling. Cool for at least 5 minutes before serving.

Zucchini Pizza Bites

2 zucchini, cut into circles or lengthwise for long strips

2 tablespoons olive oil

½ cup marinara sauce

½ cup of mozzarella cheese or nutritional yeast for dairy-free option

salt and pepper

Cut zucchini about ¼ inch thick. Toss in a bowl with olive oil and season with salt and pepper. Broil or grill for about 2 minutes on each side. Top with sauce and cheese and broil for an additional minute or two, being careful not to burn the cheese.

Grilled Zucchini

2 zucchini cut into strips like french fries

1 lime, juiced

1 tablespoon olive oil

2 tablespoons honey

1 teaspoon red pepper flakes

2 teaspoons cumin

½ teaspoon salt

½ teaspoon pepper

Mix ingredients together in a bowl. Marinate zucchini for about half of an hour. Grill or broil for about 5 minutes, until tender and soft.

BLUEBERRIES

Oh, blueberry season, how I love you.

Living in Tallahassee for 14 years and having access to lots of local blueberry farmers spoiled me rotten. The soil in Tallahassee is really great for growing blueberries because it is acidic. It's the same reason azaleas do so well there; in fact, blueberries are in the azalea family.

It's easy to grow blueberries if you have the right soil. They need lots of sun and well-drained soil that is acidic. So, the easiest thing to do is dig a big hole and put a bunch of pine bark at the bottom of the hole, and then fill in the hole after planting with nutrient-dense, well-drained soil.

You need to plant a couple different varieties side by side so they can cross-pollinate and fertilize one another. And to elongate your harvest season, plant some early varieties and some late varieties. Don't expect blueberries for several years and pinch off flower buds so they don't grow the first couple of years. You need the plant to send all it's energy to their roots and make sure they are strong and established before they start sending energy to the stems to make blueberries.

Blueberries make great yard bushes. In Tallahassee, not only did we have a 30 x 10 foot garden, we had blueberry plants and plum trees planted in our yard. I wanted to make the best and most efficient use of space in our backyard and only plants things that would produce food for us as well as look good.

They will also do pretty well in a really big container. Like the big containers for trees, choose one at least 2 x 2 x 2 feet or bigger. Ask your local nursery for blueberry varieties that do well in containers in your area.

Much like strawberries, blueberries are very high in antioxidants. Along with an anti-aging compound known as resveratrol, studies show that blueberries have a profound impact on blood regulation and increased cognitive function. While blueberries have a wide range of micronutrients, they are relatively low in amounts.

Blueberries freeze really well. Just arrange them on a baking sheet and flash freeze them for about 20 minutes and then dump them into a freezer bag. This way they won't stick together and freeze as a huge clump.

I usually buy about 15 pounds of blueberries from a local farm and freeze them all and use them throughout the year. I usually never make it all the way until the next season, I need to get another deep freezer if I wanted to do that, but I make it 75% of the year without having to buy blueberries out of season that are shipped from Chile, that don't taste half as good.

Blueberry Vinaigrette

¼ cup frozen blueberries

1 garlic clove, minced

1 tablespoon olive oil

1 tablespoon maple syrup

2 tablespoons raw apple cider vinegar

2 tablespoons balsamic vinegar

Salt & pepper to taste

Mash blueberries. Whisk ingredients together, or dump into a mason jar and give it a good shake. An even simpler and faster recipe for would be just olive oil, apple cider vinegar, mashed blueberries, and salt and pepper.

Blueberries freeze well.

Arrange them on a baking sheet and freeze them for 20 minutes, then store in a freezer bag.

Oma's Blueberry Pie

This is a favorite in my husband's mother's family. It is at least four generations old and I really enjoyed when my mother-in-law taught me how to make it. I have since adjusted the crust recipe to make it grain free, but it is just as good.

For pie crust:

1 stick unsalted butter, or ½ cup of coconut oil or lard

2 cups self-rising flour (or 2 cups all purpose gluten-free flour or almond flour)

¾ cup coconut sugar

1 whole egg

For filling:

1 pound blueberries

Sprinkling of coconut sugar

Mix all the ingredients for the pie crust by hand in a bowl. When all the ingredients are mixed, form a smooth ball, take out and roll over a piece of freezer paper until is nice and smooth. Press dough into an oiled pie pan and make sure it's pressed in evenly.

Put some breadcrumbs on top if you are using regular white flour, just a thing layer that covers all the dough. The breadcrumbs soak up the moisture from the fruit, so the crust is not soggy. If you're going the grain-free route, don't worry about the breadcrumbs; the texture will not be the same, but the taste will and you'll be able to sleep better at night because you ate so healthy!

Save some of the dough to make the pie crust top. Add the blueberries into the pie pan. Sprinkle with sugar. Then add rest of dough to make pie crust top. It does not need a top if you don't want though.

TOMATOES

Make a trip to the farmers' market during tomato season and you will find some of the best-tasting tomatoes you've ever had. Two words you'll see around the market: **Heirloom** (which means the tomatoes are not genetically modified) and **Organic** (which means they were not sprayed with chemicals or fertilizers). Not all local farmers are certified organic. The certification can be very costly for some small farmers, so they may act like Certified Organic farmers but they are just not certified. That's why it's best to make trips out to small farms and see for yourself how the vegetables are grown and animals are cared for. Although, I have yet to meet a lying farmer. I like to think that this is the kind of food my great-grandmother grew up eating before things got crazy in the industrialized farming world.

The first year I grew tomatoes was my best year. I had so many to harvest and they were all in perfect condition. I canned mountains of tomato sauce and had plenty leftover for fresh salads, snacks, and as a fresh sides at dinner. That first year had me thinking I was bad-ass gardener. But then reality hit, coming in the forms of bugs, cracked tomato skins, blight, and plants that just didn't produce. Newsflash: Tomatoes are really, really hard to grow. Even still, I plant them every year, experimenting with different heirloom varieties and planting them in different locations in my garden. I tell you all of this to make sure that you don't get discouraged with tomatoes. Keep plugging along each year and remember that gardening really is a lifelong experiment and it's all part of the fun.

Here are some tips that I've figured out along the way about tomatoes; these will get you started off on the right foot: Wait to plant seedlings until the nights are in the 50s and the days are in the 70s—that is perfect tomato weather. I learned in North Florida to get my tomatoes in the ground sometime between Valentine's Day and Easter. Here in South Florida, that means I don't plant tomatoes until the late fall! When you first start gardening tomatoes, get mature seedlings. Your success rate will be higher and you'll gain the experience you need before you start messing around growing seedlings. Another way you can build experience is by growing cherry tomatoes, which are easier to grow and can be grown indoors year-round in a sunny window.

Plant your tomato deep, up to the first bottom leaves, or even bury the first bottom stems. Once the plants get 3 feet tall, clip the bottom leaves. These leaves get the least amount of sun and are the most prone to develop diseases. Use mushroom compost and worm castings as your fertilizer and make sure your soil is very nutrient dense. Water the bottom of the plant deeply and consistently, avoiding the leaves as they don't like to get wet. Inconsistent watering will lead to rot and cracking of the tomato. Once the fruit begins to set, back off on watering a little bit.

Tomatoes are best known as a source of lycopene, an antioxidant on par with the power of carotene. In particular, lycopene has been shown to be protective against UV rays and can even help heal skin after burns. Due to the wide range of varieties of tomatoes across the globe, levels of micronutrients have been shown to be inaccurate. Nonetheless, tomatoes are still frequently cited with maintaining heart health, fighting cancers, and protecting against neurodegenerative diseases. For anyone with inflammation issues, moderation should be exercised as tomatoes are part of the nightshade family.

In the summer, I like to eat fresh tomatoes with breakfast, lunch, and dinner! When cooking with tomatoes, remember their flavor is enhanced by sugar and salt. If you freeze or can your own tomato sauce, you can get the price down to about $1 to 2 a jar, which is better than the $6 to 8 organic tomato sauce at the store!

Minestrone Soup

12 ripe tomatoes, seeded and diced

1 large onion, chopped

4 carrots, peeled and chopped

2 celery stalks, chopped

8 garlic cloves, minced

2 teaspoons fennel seeds

4 teaspoons dried sage

1 teaspoon red pepper flakes

4 teaspoons salt

6 cups of chicken broth

Optional: rind of parmigiano reggiano cheese, and some fresh shredded cheese for garnish.

Combine all ingredients (except chicken broth, beans, and cheese) into two separate gallon-sized freezer bags. Lay flat and place in freezer.

On the day of cooking, place contents of bags into your slow cooker and add chicken broth and beans and rind of parmigiano reggiano cheese. Cook on low for 8 hours or on high for 4. Add some more cheese for garnish, if you want.

Slow Cooker Tomato Meat Sauce

2 pounds ground beef

10 tomatoes, scalded and peeled

2 cups celery, finely chopped

3 cups onions, finely chopped

3 large green bell peppers, finely chopped

6 cloves garlic, crushed

2 cups mushrooms, chopped

2 6-ounce jars tomato paste

Pinch of each: Italian seasoning, garlic salt, parsley, basil, oregano, crushed red pepper

To prepare tomatoes: dunk tomato in boiling water for 1 minute, then immediately immerse in ice water. The skin will slide right off. Cut tomato in half and squeeze out the seeds (don't worry about getting every last seed). No need to chop, they will break down as they cook.

Cook onion and celery in a pan 4 to 5 minutes with meat (you can make this same recipe without meat if you'd like). Combine all ingredients in a crock pot and simmer on low for 8 to 10 hours. Taste and season as needed. Once sauce has cooled, freeze in individual freezer bags or mason jars (be careful to fill it up and leave ½ inch of room at the top) and thaw slowly, so you don't break your mason jar.

Caprese Salad

3 tomatoes

1 bunch basil

1 pound mozzarella

Salt to taste

Pepper to taste

Fig vinegar or organic cold pressed olive oil

Learn more online!

Slice the tomato and the fresh mozzarella as evenly as possible, cutting slowly with a serrated knife. Salt the tomato and layer it with cheese and basil in one long row or in stacks. You can also chop up all the ingredients and serve in a bowl, or cut ingredients into small pieces and skewer with toothpicks for bite-sized appetizers. Once you have assembled the ingredients the way you want, add a tiny bit more salt and pepper. Then drizzle with fig vinegar (I get this from Turkey Hill Farm—it is amazing and goes great with anything!) or a really high-quality, organic, cold-pressed olive oil. And that's it! Take a bite and dive into a very yummy and healthy summer salad!

> Watermelons help replenish fluids and electrolytes during hot summer days and have been shown to lower blood pressure.

July: Watermelon and Figs

WATERMELON

Despite having significant sugar content, watermelon is actually low in calories due to its very high water content. True to its name, watermelon is an excellent fruit during hot summer days to replenish fluids and electrolytes. While not notably high in micronutrients, watermelon does have large amounts of lycopene and carotenoids. Possibly acting on the mild diuretic properties, watermelon has been shown to lower blood pressure.

Native to Africa, melons need warm temperatures (up to 80 degrees during the day) and a long growing season. Gardeners in colder climates can still have success in growing watermelon by starting seeds indoors and choosing short-season varieties. Days to maturity range from 70 to 90, depending on the variety.

Amend soil with aged manure or compost before planting. Growing the vines in raised rows, known as hills, ensures good drainage and will hold the sun's heat longer. If you are in a cooler zone, start seeds indoors about a month before transplanting. Watermelon vines are very tender and should not be transplanted until all danger of frost has passed. If you live in warmer climes, you can direct sow seeds outdoors, but wait until the soil temperature warms to at least 65 degrees to avoid poor germination. Space the plants about 2 feet apart in a 5-foot-wide hill.

While melon plants are growing, blooming, and setting fruit, they need 1 to 2 inches of water per week. Water in the morning and try to avoid wetting the leaves. Reduce watering once fruit are growing. Dry weather produces the sweetest melon.

I buy a whole watermelon instead of the pre-cut portions to save money. Even though it is so tempting to have someone else do the prep work for me and I always worry that I am going to waste some of the melon. I usually cut up a few slices to eat fresh and cut up the rest to put in the freezer as melon popsicles. I like to add watermelon to fresh salads in the summer and add flavors like lemon and feta cheese. Or make watermelon water with mint leaves for a refreshing sweet drink that doesn't have sugar or dyes, or other yucky stuff, in it.

Watermelon Popsicles

½ large watermelon

popsicle sticks (you can get them at any craft store)

Cut watermelon into small triangles or into shapes using a cookie cutter. Push a lollipop stick into each piece and lay on a cookie sheet lined with freezer paper and place in freezer, or freeze the pieces of watermelon without the popsicle using the same method. Serve frozen.

Chilled Watermelon Soup

1-inch piece of ginger, peeled and finely chopped

2 limes, one for zest and both for juice

4 cups watermelon, cubed and seeded

2 mint leaves, plus more for garnish

¼ cup plus 2 tablespoons filtered water

In a small skillet, gently sauté ginger and zest in 2 tablespoons water over medium heat for 2 minutes. Add lime juice and simmer until no liquid remains. Transfer mixture to a blender (or to a big bowl and use an immersion blender) and add watermelon, mint, and water. Puree until smooth; strain with sieve into bowl to remove all the seeds. Chill soup at least 3 hours. Garnish with mint leaves before serving.

FIGS

Figs are native to Asia and the Mediterranean where they have grown since 5,000 B.C. They are surprisingly high in calcium and fiber. Although dried figs are more common for their concentrated health benefits, the fresh variety still have many benefits, such as B vitamins, potassium, copper, and iron. Despite the fact that figs are quite sweet, they have been shown to have a positive effect on blood glucose levels. Be wary of eating too many as they can act as a laxative.

Fig trees thrive in dry, warm weather. They are beautiful; compact trees with big leaves and would make a great yard tree if they grow well in your area. Fig trees adapt to a variety of soil types, including rich loam, clay, or light sands. The trees do not grow well in very acidic soils and prefer a pH of 6.0 to 6.5. Fig trees tolerate moderate levels of salinity. Fig trees do really well in Tallahassee for the same reason blueberries do.

Fresh, in-season figs are quite the treat. Fresh figs are great with goat cheese on a grain-free cracker (check out my blog for a great recipe!) or Mary's Gone Crackers, and great on a pizza with onions, goat cheese, and a fig vinaigrette. If you freeze them, be prepared to only use them in recipes that you will mush them up anyway, like a pie. Some people eat the skin, but I like to peel them (it's a pain in the butt).

Fig Pie

Exactly the same as the blueberry pie found on page 35 but with figs!

August: Peaches and Eggplant

PEACHES

Peaches are a popular tree for home gardens because they self-pollinate, meaning you only need one tree. If you don't have a strong bee population in your area, it is suggested you take a paint brush when the flowers open and dabble it in each one, basically doing the work of bees to ensure a good crop. When the peaches get to the size of marble, thin out the fruit to a maximum of three per stem. This ensures there is not stunted growth and also that the stem will not break from the weight of too many peaches.

Peaches are a part of the stone fruit family, because of the hard pit at the center. Nectarines are a close cousin of the peach, but without the fuzz on its skin. Peaches are one of the few plants to contain any significant amount of fluoride. Unlike chemically produced fluoride compounds added to water and toothpastes, naturally occurring fluoride does aid in bone and dental health. Although they contain potassium, iron, and vitamin C as well, peaches are not a good source for micronutrients.

Quick-cooking peaches on the grill brings out their natural juiciness and intensifies their deep summer sweetness. Peaches with goat cheese, basil, and walnuts are delicious. Oftentimes, I will grill a ton of chicken breasts at once and then freeze them. All I have to do on a night I need an easy dinner is take out three pieces of chicken and make whatever vegetable side I want. I freeze peaches in small bags to add to the grill or sauté for a quick side.

Peach Baby Back Ribs

Visit my blog for my BBQ sauce recipe and how to cook Baby Back Ribs.

To include peaches, simply add melted butter, ghee, or coconut oil to peaches and mix together in a bowl. Grill peaches until they are heated through with grill lines. Season peaches with pepper and serve with Baby Back Ribs.

Peach Vegetable Stir Fry

3 peaches, cut into sixths

1 pound green beans (or snow peas, but green beans are in season at the same time)

2 inches of ginger, peeled and chopped

4 garlic cloves, minced

2 tablespoons butter

1 tablespoon sugar

2 tablespoons tamari sauce

Melt butter in a skillet and add in ginger, garlic, and green beans, and cook for about 5 minutes. Add in peaches, tamari sauce, and sugar, and cook until peaches are soft and flavors have melded.

EGGPLANT

I love growing eggplant. They like really hot weather so it's always my best producer in August when the Florida heat can be too much for other vegetables. Eggplant requires 100 to 140 warm days with temperatures consistently between 70 and 90 degrees to reach harvest. Same as with other homegrown vegetables, eggplant tastes way better than something bought at the store, especially if bought out of season. No bitterness, just bursting with hearty flavor. When you buy an eggplant at the grocery store, buy one that is smooth and unmarked with a fresh-looking green cap. They look sturdy, but they go bad in the fridge very quickly (another great reason to garden), so plan to cook your eggplant the day of purchase (or picking), or next day. You can pull them the day you want to cook them!

Set eggplants into the garden 18 to 24 inches apart; they get big so give them some space. Plant eggplants away from tomatoes and corn but close to bush beans, southern peas, and nitrogen-fixing crops. I put a cage around my eggplants to help keep them upright, as they can get heavy and can use a little extra help. Eggplants are ready for harvest when the fruit is glossy, firm, and full colored and not streaked with brown. Time from planting to harvest is 100 to 150 days from seed, 70 to 85 days from transplants. The eggplant fruit grows on a sturdy stem; cut the fruit from the stem with a sharp knife.

Eggplants are fairly unremarkable in micronutrient quantities. As part of the nightshade family (which also includes bell peppers and tomatoes), moderation should be exercised for individuals with inflammation problems. The most surprising part about eggplants is that they actually contain nicotine; however, levels are negligible and it would take about 20 pounds to be equivalent to a single cigarette. Despite that, studies have shown that they can contribute to lowering blood cholesterol levels.

Eggplant is substantial, with an almost meaty texture. On the nights I want vegetarian fare, eggplant is filling for me and my meat-and-potatoes-loving husband. In fact, the first time I served him my grain-free eggplant parmesan, he asked, "Are you sure there is no meat in this?"

When cooking eggplant, don't forget to salt and sweat them before cooking. This means that after slicing, you want to line them on a towel and salt them a bit and let the bitter juices seep out.

Grain-Free Eggplant Parmesan

2 medium eggplants, cut into ½-inch-thick round slices

½ teaspoon sea salt

1 tablespoon olive oil

½ teaspoon oregano

½ teaspoon thyme

½ teaspoon black pepper

3 cups almond flour

2 tablespoons cooking fat

3 eggs

½ cup each Mozzarella and Parmesan cheese

2 tablespoons whole raw milk or coconut milk

1 jar (16 ounces) marinara sauce

Arrange eggplant slices on paper towels and sprinkle with a little sea salt and let the bitter juices seep out for about an hour. Mix together dry ingredients in one bowl, and egg and milk in another bowl. Heat olive oil in frying pan. Dredge an eggplant slice with the egg/milk mixture and then the dry ingredients, then fry it. Repeat until all the slices are cooked. Then layer eggplant slices, marinara sauce and cheese in a pan (I use a glass Pyrex one) until your dish is full, cheese topping last. Then bake in the oven at 350 degrees for 30 minutes.

Grilled Eggplant

1 large eggplant, cut into ½-inch-thick round slices

1 big bunch arugula

6 ounces fontina cheese

extra virgin olive oil

sea salt

1 loaf sourdough bread (if you want to make sandwiches)

Spread out eggplant slices on a towel and sprinkle with sea salt, letting stand for about an hour to get all the bitter juices out. Brush both sides of eggplant with olive oil and grill over medium high heat for 4 minutes on each side. Add a slice of cheese to each round of eggplant and remove from heat after about 1 minute; the residual heat will melt the cheese. Serve on a bed of arugula or, if you'd like a sandwich, place eggplant and lots of arugula leaves between two slices of bread.

Fall

Fall has always been my favorite time of year. I love the fall foliage and the cooler weather. It always seems to calm and ground me. **I am normally hot blooded and hot tempered**, so fall seems to put me in check and I feel the most calm and centered.

September: Okra and Bell Peppers

OKRA

Okra is a fun plant to grow. They grow pretty tall and attractive with the finger-like okras hanging down, looking kind of like a Christmas tree. I have seen farms make okra trellis/arches so that you walk down the middle of the row under a canopy of okra.

I first learned about growing okra from a childhood best friend. Her parents own a small organic farm in Georgia and, on a visit during the summer, I helped harvest some okra and we cooked succotash. I remember how good it felt to go out to their garden and pick a vegetable for dinner. And I tucked away the mental notes I took on that trip because I knew that one day I would be living that lifestyle, too, where I could cook with whatever was on hand in the garden.

Regardless of how it is cooked, okra has mucous-like fiber that significantly aids digestion. Being especially high in folate, vitamin C, calcium, and potassium, okra makes for an incredible health food.

BELL PEPPERS

Unlike other peppers, bell peppers contain only a small amount of the heat-producing compound capsaicin. Despite that, this important alkaloid has anti-bacterial, anti-carcinogenic, and analgesic properties. All bell peppers have significant amounts of vitamin C; however, red peppers contain the highest source of nutrients over other varieties, including lycopene and carotene.

Bell peppers are kind of flimsy plants and I usually stake them just like eggplants and tomatoes. Don't wait for your green peppers to get as huge as you normally see in the grocery store; in my experience, they should be picked when they are about the size of your fist. Last year, we had such a great crop of heirloom purple bell peppers, and it was wonderful.

I try to cook as many as I can fresh, but freezing bell peppers is a great option. Simply cut them how you want, diced or in slices, and freeze them in a gallon-sized freezer bag.

Succotash

1 cup chopped okra

1 cup chopped green pepper

1 cup chopped onion

1 cup chopped tomato

3 garlic cloves, chopped

2 tablespoons butter or bacon grease

Use equal amounts of everything, except cooking fat and garlic. The order of sautéing is important because some veggies take longer to cook than others. Start with the corn, onions, and green peppers, and then add the garlic, tomatoes, and okra.

Succotash traditionally includes beans or peas. I like it better without, but you can certainly add peas or beans into this recipe if you want. Please note if you are grain free, leave out the corn. It is traditional to cook this meal with corn; however, it still tastes wonderful without it, I just add more bell peppers to give it the same crunch corn would give to it.

October: Grapes and Apples

GRAPES

My husband's aunt and uncle live in Argentina. At their house, they have gorgeous grapevines growing over a pergola on their back porch. Around 7 years ago, we visited them and I was amazed by all the bunches of grapes hanging down everywhere! They were so pretty! His cousin Mateo, a baby at the time, was just learning to talk. He would point and shout, "Uba! Uba!" at the grapes. He would also call his Grandpa "Uba" because of the glass of wine he always had in his hand. My husband's aunt makes all kinds of grape pies and jams that taste as amazing as you'd imagine.

Grapes grow well in many areas, but each area has a variety that does well. In North Florida, muscadine grapes grow the best. Grapes can be a rewarding backyard crop, as established vines have few pests and remain fruitful for decades. A single vine can produce 15 to 20 pounds of grapes each year, typically from August to October depending on the area. The easiest way to tell if your grapes are ready is by tasting them each as harvest time nears. They develop their full color weeks before they are actually ready so the only way to know is by a taste test!

Plant grapes in the spring on sturdy posts 6 to 8 feet apart. They need weekly watering the first three years and, like blueberries, you need to pinch off fruit for the first three years so the roots can become well established.

Many of the touted health benefits of wine actually come directly from the grapes themselves. High in a polyphenol called resveratrol, this anti-aging compound fights cancers, heart disease, neurological conditions, and even viruses and fungal infections. Grapes contain a variety of other polyphenols, each with their own health-promoting benefits.

Unwashed grapes stored in a cluster inside an airtight container will last a full week or more. Some flavor combinations I love for grapes are either chicken or fish with tarragon, or alongside blue cheese or mint.

Waldorf Salad

6 apples, cored and diced (granny smith and ambrosia work best)

2 pounds red or green grapes (or mix of both)

1 cup chopped walnuts

½ cup shredded coconut

½ cup of mayonnaise

½ cup of orange juice

Chop apples, grapes, and walnuts. Mix all ingredients together in a bowl. Serve cold.

Roasted Chicken with Grapes and Onions

4 boneless, skinless chicken breasts, rinsed and dried

2 onions, quartered

1 cup red seedless grapes

2 tablespoons dijon mustard

1 tablespoon balsamic vinegar

1 tablespoon olive oil

½ cup coconut milk keifer

1 cup almond meal/flour

¼ teaspoon salt

Preheat oven to 350 degrees. Combine mustard, vinegar, and coconut milk keifer, and coat chicken pieces completely and roll in almond meal. Arrange chicken in a large baking dish. In a bowl, gently toss onions and grapes with oil to coat, add to baking dish and sprinkle everything with salt and pepper. Bake until chicken is crisp and golden and internal temperature is 165 degrees.

APPLES

Apples have a long harvest season, so it's possible to harvest apples from August to November, depending on your area. They are certainly found at a great price at farmers' markets and grocery stores during that same time period. Your farmers' market is far more likely to have tasty, and heritage varieties that are unique and delicious. Penelope had her first experience picking apples on a recent trip to visit friends that recently moved to the Asheville, NC area and it was so fun. I hope we can make a trip up every year.

Despite the large variety of apples, they almost universally have shown to improve health, primarily through the consumption of the apple skin. The skin contains ursolic acid, which has been linked with building healthy fat stores, and decreasing unhealthy fat stores, including liver fat. The apple skin itself also contains many other phytochemicals and antioxidants that aid the body in clearing cancers.

Apples for eating will be good in the fridge for up to 6 weeks; if you are going to use them for cooking, they will keep for three months! Apples go great with blue cheese in a winter salad.

Apple Grilled Cheese Sandwiches

1 apple, peeled and sliced

3 slices bacon

4 slices bread, preferably a homemade sourdough or something made with a soaked, sprouted whole grains, or a gluten-free/grain-free bread

8 ounces of cheddar cheese

bacon grease

Cook bacon then set aside. Add slices of bread to hot grease. Add cheese on one slice of bread and apples and bacon on the other. When the bread has browned, press slices together. I used my cast-iron teapot to press it down, but if you have some sort of panini press, that would work well. Make sure to wipe the bottom of whatever you are using to press the sandwich or the bacon grease will burn the crap out of it the next time you use it.

Bread-free alternative: melt cheese on apple slices in a toaster oven or on the skillet for 30 seconds.

I made these sandwiches (minus the bacon slices) for my daughter's fall apple themed 2nd birthday party. They were snatched up by children and adults alike, and were gone in minutes. They make for a great lunch or snack and freeze really well.

Chicken Curry Salad

2 cups chicken, chopped (either baked chicken breasts or leftovers from a roasted chicken)

1 vidalia or other sweet onion, chopped

2 ribs celery, chopped

2 apples diced

½ cup pecans

½ cup raisins

½ cup mayonnaise

2 teaspoons curry powder

Chop ingredients and mix up everything together in a bowl and served chilled. Eat as a sandwich, on crackers, or on top of a bed of salad greens.

November: Pomegranates, Cranberries, and Pumpkins

My daughter Penelope was born in November . . . 11/11 to be exact, and now, in addition to fall being my favorite season, November is my favorite month.

POMEGRANATES

Pomegranates are native to southeastern Europe and Asia and have been cultivated in ancient Egypt, Babylonia, India, and Iran. The Spanish brought them to Mexico, California, and Arizona in the 16th Century. They are easy to grow, have beautiful flowers, and are well suited to the desert climate.

I have never grown pomegranates because they don't grow well in Florida, but I do only eat them when they are in season. Here are some quick tips on selecting the right ones from the farmers' market or grocery store when they are in season:

- Choose a large pomegranate as it will typically have juicier seeds (arils).
- Choose a heavy pomegranate as it will typically have more juice.
- Look for fruit with a supple leathery skin. Dry skin signals the fruit is drying out. Also check that there are no blemishes, as a damaged exterior may signal a damaged interior.
- The color should be deep red, as lighter-skinned ones are not as good.
- Look at the shape. Pomegranates will never be perfectly round, but any flat spots may indicate that an inner membrane has dried out.

An untouched pomegranate will keep for three months in a fridge. Seeds will last in an airtight container for 3 to 4 days. The interior of a pomegranate contains as many as 800 seeds encased in sacs full of juice known as arils, which are held in place by membranes. Much like grapes, pomegranates are packed with polyphenols. The fruit is particularly popular with Ayurvedic medicine, and due to its popularity in eastern medicine, pomegranate juice is currently being run through a variety of studies for its use in cancer fighting, heart disease, and diabetes. I ate a lot of pomegranate during late pregnancy and early postpartum. I did not want to give my daughter any shots, including a vitamin K shot, so I beefed up on eating food that had vitamin K in it, which means that I ate a lot of pomegranate seeds. It's no wonder that Penelope's favorite fruit is pomegranate seeds!

Pomegranate Salad

1 big bunch of arugula

2 cups pomegranate seeds

1 apple, chopped

1 shallot, minced

2 lemons, juiced

2 tablespoons olive oil

salt and pepper to taste

Chop apple and shallot, deseed pomegranates, and juice lemons. Mix everything together in a big bowl.

How to Seed a Pomegranate

Getting the seeds out of a pomegranate can be a little bit of a pain, but here are a few tips to make it easy:

1 Score the pomegranate into quarters or sixths and place in a big bowl of water.

2 Break open the pomegranates under water to free the arils. The arils will sink to the bottom of the bowl and the membrane will float to the top.

3 Scoop out the membrane with a spoon—if you leave the pomegranate to soak for too long, the membrane will fall to the bottom.

PUMPKINS

Close cousins, squash and pumpkins are easy to grow. They require very little care, which makes them an excellent first crop for beginners and children. They need 6 to 8 hours of full sun each day and well-drained garden soil. Plant in clusters of three so they can cross-pollinate and fertilize one another. Like peaches, you can take a paint brush and dabble each flower to make sure cross-pollination happens, in case the bees in your area are lacking (due to pesticides and other environmental factors killing them off). To attract bees to your garden, plant zinnias and calendula flowers.

Pumpkins make lots of vines and will take up a lot of room in your garden, so be prepared to give up plenty of space in your garden for them to grow. You should build up one big mound of dirt about 2 feet high, and plant about 6 seeds, 6 inches apart, with the pointy side of the seed facing down towards the earth. I actually like to grow pumpkins in an empty corner of my yard to really let it grow big and not sacrifice space in my garden.

Pumpkins are ready for harvest when it is hard to scratch the skin with your fingernail. Once a pumpkin is ready, you want it to cure for another 10 to 20 days outside. Curing will harden the rinds and sweeten up the pumpkin on the inside. Once cured, bring it inside for storage. They will keep for many months in a cool, dark place at about 70 degrees.

Both pumpkin flesh and pumpkin seeds have potent health benefits. Pumpkin flesh in particular is known for digestive health promoting fiber, so it is commonly prescribed to dogs, cats, and even chickens. Some phytochemicals found in pumpkins are undergoing research as a means to help control insulin levels.

To cook your own pumpkins, get the small pumpkins, usually called pie or sweet pumpkins. Look for ones that are firm with no bruising. Cut them in half, spoon out the seeds and roast them in the oven for about 30 minutes or until soft. Once cool, spoon out the meat and then trash or compost the skins. Every fall I cook a huge batch of pumpkins when they are in season, and puree them and freeze them in 2 cup portions. That way I can pull a bag out of my freezer for whatever fall recipe I am making the next year.

A note about canned foods: You can use a can of cooked pumpkin if you really want to, but even organic food cans have BPA in them, so I avoid them whenever possible.

Leftover Turkey Soup

Leftover meat from turkey

2 medium carrots

2 stalks celery

1 medium onion

2 cloves garlic

2 medium potatoes

1 bunch kale

1 cup french lentils

4 cups chicken or turkey stock

1 teaspoon basil

1 teaspoon thyme

1 teaspoon oregano

1 bay leaf

salt and pepper to taste

Sauté the carrots, celery, and onion (known as mirepoix) in butter. Add everything else and bring to a boil for a few minutes, then turn heat to low. Cover and simmer until veggies are tender, about an hour.

This is a good amount of food, so I use a large 5-quart sauté pan. And just FYI, simmering is a great way to keep the meat tender and get the most nutrients from the vegetables.

Pumpkin Soup

2 medium pumpkins, seeded and cubed

2 medium onions, chopped

2 tablespoons cooking fat

6 cups chicken stock (added day of cooking)

1 cup heavy cream or coconut milk (added in after cooking, before serving)

1 teaspoon rosemary

1 teaspoon thyme

1 teaspoon sage

2 cinnamon sticks

2 bay leaves

Heat butter in a large pan and sauté onions, then pumpkins. When onions are translucent, add stock and spices and bring to a boil for a few minutes. Turn heat to low and simmer for several hours. Just before serving, add in heavy cream and use immersion blender to puree soup to desired consistency. Adding more stock if you want the soup to have a thinner consistency.

Roasted Pumpkin Seeds

First, get all your seeds out of the pumpkin with a spoon. Get all the strings of pumpkin meat off and give them a good rinse. Then put them a bowl of warm water with salt and let them soak for 24 hours (to reduce phytic acid that bind nutrients in your digestive system). Once they are done, drain them and put them on a baking sheet. Salt them some more and roast them in the oven at 350 degrees for about 15 minutes, or until they start to brown and crisp up.

I like to go the traditional route of just roasting my pumpkin seeds with sea salt so that if I decide to add them to a salad or other recipe, I have flexibility to flavor the dish as I want.

If you want to spice things up, you can try this spicy roasted pumpkin seed recipe:

1 cup pumpkin seeds

1 teaspoon chili powder

½ teaspoon cayenne pepper

½ teaspoon coarse salt

3 teaspoons fresh lime juice

CRANBERRIES

Contrary to popular understanding, cranberries aren't actually grown in flooded bogs or marshes. Cranberry fields are flooded to make harvesting easier (the berries float) but that is not how they grow all season long. And this is a method used for commercial growers, not your average home gardener. You simply have to pick the berries by hand. There is no need to flood your cranberry patch.

I have never grown cranberries, but there is no real reason an ambitious home gardener couldn't do it. You can buy cuttings or seedlings to start your berry field. The plants will start to produce fruit at around 3 years of age. So, a year-old cutting will take some time before you harvest, whereas a 3-year old seedling will give you fruit almost immediately during the first fall after planting. Pick your cranberry harvest before the frost hits in late fall when the berries are deep red, and the seed inside is brown.

Before winter sets in, put a heavy layer of mulch over your plants (extra pine needles, if you have them). You can uncover them in early spring, but they will need to be recovered any night you are expecting frost.

Cranberries are quite particular about their soil, so don't feel you can skimp on this or try to make do with regular yard dirt. Most gardeners dig out a bed and replace it with the right mixture rather than try to amend their existing soil. Take out the existing topsoil in your cranberry bed (4 feet by 8 feet is an average size) to a depth of about 6 to 8 inches. Fill in your bed with peat moss, and then mix in about a half pound of bone meal, and a full pound of blood meal for nutrients. Wet the whole bed down well before putting in your seedlings.

Cranberries are high in vitamin C and antioxidants. Best known for its juice aide in treatment of urinary tract infections, cranberries are another fruit very high in antioxidant properties. Not only does it help with the urinary tract in a variety of ways, it can also help prevent tooth decay by the same method of killing bacteria. This fruit filled with tart tannins has also been shown to help control blood glucose and kidney stone formation.

Cranberries can last longer than most berries and will taste as good as fresh after 2 months in the fridge if stored in a tightly sealed container. Once cooked, they can keep for a month in the fridge, too. Dried cranberries are a treat with a texture similar to a raisin. When cooking with cranberries, adding just a tiny amount of honey or natural sugar will cut the tartness and enhance the flavor.

Homemade Cranberry Sauce

2 pounds or 2 bags of cranberries

1 cup of sugar or honey, or to taste

Bring about 2 inches of water to boil and then add in cranberries. It takes about 15 minutes to cook them down. They will pop as they cook and then turn mushy. Take off the heat and add sugar or honey. Let cool and then add to sandwich-sized freezer bags, 12 to 15 ounces in each bag. I don't add any spices to my cranberry sauce so that I can add them to whatever meal I am making and add the spices then and change up the flavors.

Thanks for reading!

As the Founder and Creative Director of Mama and Baby Love—once a yoga studio and eco-friendly boutique and now a thriving website about real food, natural living, motherhood, and healing—thank you for purchasing and using my cookbook.

As a mother, healer, mentor, and businesswoman, I care deeply about nourishing and loving myself so that I can nourish and love my family. It means so much to me to be able to share helpful information with other mothers. I truly hope the recipes in this cookbook help you nourish and love yourself and your own families and help you on your journey to being the healthiest, happiest mother you can be.

You may also be interested in:

M+BL's From Your Freezer To Your Family

M+BL's Gluten-Free Grain-Free Baking

Gluten-Free Grain-Free

BAKING

A healthy baking cookbook for mamas who don't know how to bake.

Stephanie Brandt Cornais

Gluten-free/Grain-free Baking Cookbook for Beginners

Copyright © 2013 by Nourish & Love, LLC. All rights reserved. No part of this publication may be reproduced or transmitted in any form or by any means, electronic or mechanical, including photocopying, recording or by any information storage and retrieval system, without permission in writing from the Publisher.

Inquiries or requests to the the Publisher for permission should be sent addressed to:

Stephanie Brandt Cornais
3801 Piney Grove Drive
Tallahassee, Fl 32311

info@MamaAndBabyLove.com

Produced by Nourish & Love, LLC
Photographs © 2012 Stephanie Brandt Cornais
Recipe © 2012 Stephanie Brandt Cornais

Nutrition Editor: Cassandra Roy
Content Editor: Josh Sampiero - youneedjosh.com

Designed by Jessica Barnard, The Pixelista - thepixelista.com

chapter outline

My Baking Story 1

Why Bake Differently? 3

Baking Tips and Tricks 4

Quality Ingredients 8

Cookies 12

Cakes 17

Pies 21

Pizza Crusts 23

Icings 25

About the Author 27

Hi, I'm Stephanie, and that's my daughter, Penelope. When she was 6 months old, I started planning for her 1st birthday. I was determined to bake sugar cookies and ice them with royal icing. I had pictures from Martha Stewart magazine up in my kitchen for inspiration. I must have done a bajillion trial runs in the months leading up to her birthday, but every time I could not get the icing right. Every time they looked like a drunk person put the icing on them.

And then I gave up on perfect. I was never going to be Martha Stewart. It dawned on me that I cared more about making a healthy treat for my daughter than making a cookie that was magazine cover ready. So I switched to baking her a cake. A healthy cake. Or as healthy as a cake can be and still taste like a dang cake!

The cake was lopsided and my husband said, "Uh, it looks very homemade." but I didn't care. It tasted amazing to me. Penelope? She decided it was going to be this particular cake would become an acquired taste.

It took confidence to start baking

After success in the kitchen with my slow cooker freezer recipes, I had the courage to venture into baking. I used to say that I was a terrible baker - that I lacked the precision and attention to details to get it right. But mostly I was just afraid of messing up. Once I became more confident in the kitchen, I was willing to experiment. I no longer consider myself a bad baker. Part of that is because I am consciously choosing to change my story. I am now saying that I am learning the art of gluten-free/grain-free baking! But part of that is because to me, grain-free and gluten-free baking is just easier. No one expects it to look like a perfect Martha Stewart sugar cookie, because you are not using the standard ingredients. If it looks lumpy or doesn't rise quite right, it's okay because it's grain-free or gluten-free! I think there is much more wiggle room in grain-free/gluten-free baking.

My daughter also loves to bake with me. She gets so excited when I say it's time to bake! She runs over to her learning tower and hops in. Or she she will go to the bin where I keep my flour and start helping me get the "recipe." This has become such an important part of our mother/daughter experience. It wasn't part of my childhood – which inspires to me make sure it's part of hers.

I live by the 80/20 rule, so we are not strict grain-free, paleo, or gluten-free in our house. I just like to do more of what makes me feel good and less of what makes me feel not-so-good. But even though I occasionally eat grains or gluten, every recipe in this cookbook is gluten and grain-free, and even more importantly, easy to make. They're a way for you to start doing real grain-free and gluten-free cooking in your own home, just like I do.

> I used to say that I was a **terrible baker!** But I was just afraid to try.

Why bake differently?

Gluten sensitivity and celiac disease are some reasons people go gluten-free, but even if you don't have a sensitivity, your body has to do a lot of work to digest gluten. This takes energy away from your body functioning at the optimal levels of health. Plus, the harder your digestion system has to work to digest its food, the less nutrients you actually absorb and are able to use. Eventually your gut gets weaker and weaker from having to work so hard to digest food. That means it gets less and less good at its job, which of course leads to a whole host of health issues.

> Gluten is hard to digest – even if you're healthy!

So reducing your grain and gluten consumption is a great thing to do for your health, even if you are not 100% grain or gluten-free. Giving your digestion a break for even a small time is beneficial. If you've noticed aches and pains in your body that don't go away with chiropractic care or massage therapy, your energy level is low, or you keep feeling like you are catching a cold, try going gluten-free or grain-free for a couple of days or even longer, and I'll bet you notice a real difference.

Baking tips & tricks

To make your kitchen adventures a little less of a challenge and perhapys a tiny bit (or a lot!) more fun, I've shared a few lessons I've learned over the years.

Mind your liquids.

When swapping out white sugar for something like maple syrup, keep in mind the ratio of liquids. If you add in the liquid of the syrup, cut back on something like milk to keep things in balance.

Cream your butter and sugar for better baking - but skip it to save time.

Most recipes call for "creaming" butter and sugar together as the first step and then slowly blending in the rest of the ingredients. I am the kind of home cook that is not concerned with looks and pretty, perfect outcomes. I care way more about the fact that I managed to get my crap together for the day and make something homemade for myself and my family. So sometimes my cookies are not as fluffy, or can't be rolled out and used as cut-out cookies. But I don't care. If you care about that sort of thing, cream your butter and sugar! Work the butter and sugar in your mixer for about 8 - 10 minutes. Creaming incorporates the maximum amount of air bubbles and will make your baked good rise and be light and fluffy.

Start with the easy stuff!

If you are afraid to try baking like I was, pick the least scariest recipe to try first. It wouldn't help if I were to recommend one. They are all pretty easy as far as skill level goes, but read through this book first and then see what your gut tells you. Which one do you have the most confidence to try? Success in the kitchen in general has a lot to do with getting over your fear of messing up and experimenting. You will learn how to bake eventually, you just need to start somewhere!

Baking Tips & Tricks

Most grain-free and gluten-free flours are interchangeable.

They all pretty much work the same, it's just a matter of taste and texture preferences. I would recommend just using whatever you have on hand and going with the flow. If I have an opened package of coconut flour that I need to use up, I am not gonna open up a brand new package of something else just because a recipe calls for almond flour.

Flour ratios are standard.

If a regular recipe calls for 2 cups of all-purpose flour, you can simply swap out for gluten-free all-purpose flour or 2 cups of almond or coconut flour. Like I mentioned before, I am not seeking perfection nor do I have any desire to be exact, but if that is something you are interested in, there are more precise flour substitution information available online. For example, wheat flour generally soaks up more liquid than almond flour, so keep that in mind when looking at the ratios to wet and dry ingredients.

Be precise - when you can.

Since I am usually always baking with a 3 year old "helping" me, I am never precise when it comes to measuring flours and other ingredients. I used to not want to bake because I was so overwhelmed and worried that I had to get it perfect. But take a deep breath! It's really not that much of a science. Even with my three year old helping me and not properly scooping/leveling/weighing and doing all that fancy stuff, my recipes usually come out just fine – and even if they don't, it's not the end of the world.

Swap out oils.

As you start baking more with gluten-free and grain-free flours, and want to convert some old recipes, know that you can always swap out canola oil or vegetable oil for coconut oil and butter to make a recipe not only gluten-free but also more nutrient dense and healthier.

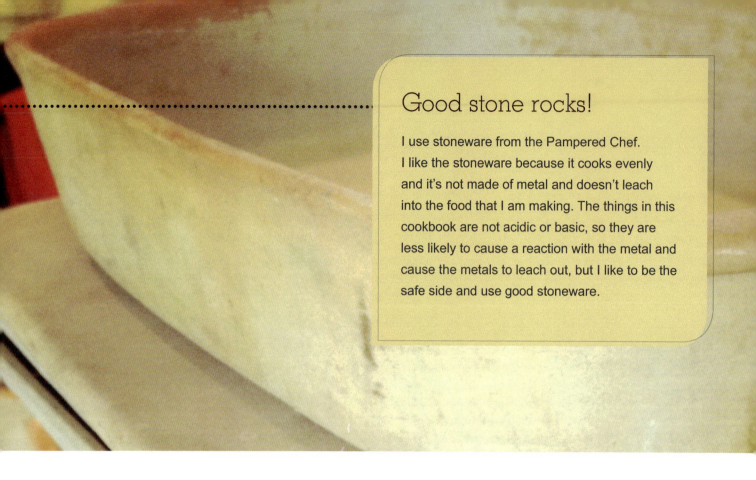

Good stone rocks!

I use stoneware from the Pampered Chef. I like the stoneware because it cooks evenly and it's not made of metal and doesn't leach into the food that I am making. The things in this cookbook are not acidic or basic, so they are less likely to cause a reaction with the metal and cause the metals to leach out, but I like to be the safe side and use good stoneware.

Baking Tips & Tricks

Preparation is key.

I like to be the mom that prepares. I once started preparing for my daughter's birthday party over a year in advance. (Call me crazy!) But sometimes, things go wrong, or something unexpected comes up. There was a time in my life where that would thrown this train completely off the tracks - but I've learned you can't plan for everything, and sometimes you've got take the bumps as they come along. When my planned-for recipe didn't work out, I knew right where to turn! A huge thanks to Paula of Lucy and Leo's Cupcakery in Tallahassee, FL, for saving the day at my daughter's birthday party with delicious, incredible gluten-free cupcakes - and for helping us out with some from-the-pros hints on how to be a great gluten-free baker, below.

4 Tips from Lucy and Leo's Cupcakery

1 Try to keep it simple. The less ingredients in the recipe, the better your recipe is going to turn out.

2 Make sure your flours are ground very fine and then sifted. This prevents that gritty, sandy texture.

3 If the final product isn't "Martha Stewart" perfect, food process it into crumbs for yummy toppings.

4 Different flours affect density, moisture and crumb. Too spongy? Hard as rock? Change flours.

I like chocolate.

...so I always double the amount of chocolate chips. If I call for a full cup of chocolate chips in a cookie recipe, it's because I love chocolate, but you could cut that back to ¼ or ½ cup if you wanted to.

Baking Tips & Tricks

Almond flour burns easily.

It's no secret you'll have to adjust some of your baking techniques to use different ingredients. Here's one thing I've learned baking with almond flour: it burns much more quickly, so you really have to watch your baked goods in the oven, and make sure that your cookies, muffins or cakes don't get a little too crispy, too quickly!

Save some for later!

I always freeze cookies and cakes after I have eaten some fresh. This way I always have a homemade baked good on hand and don't feel pressure to go out and buy them when I get a craving. I hate waste, so I used to eat them all in a day or two. Now I have a couple and stow them away in the freezer. Later, I pull them out of the freezer and simply warm them in the oven. You can freeze dough as well.

Use quality ingredients.

Whenever I bake I use the highest quality ingredients possible. All dairy is from local farms. The chocolate chips are organic and fair trade, the salt is sea salt, the vanilla is organic and sometimes homemade. Everything down to the last drop of honey is raw and local – meaning delicious.

Oils

Butter, coconut oil, palm oil (palm shortening and palm kernal oil), as well as lard are all viable options to use in baked goods if you want to treat your body right. Since they are all saturated fats, they have little difference in texture and only really show themselves in flavor. Utilizing good quality fats is important for turning an occasional sweet indulgence into an opportunity for nutrition. Not only do these fats ease the burden of ingesting sugars by slowing down glucose absorption, they also pack in additional nutrients and load you up with leptin, a hormone that triggers satiety. All three of those factors – glucose absorption, nutrients, and leptin – will help you keep the sweets to a minimum. Enjoy a treat, but without the guilt.

The Power of Flour

There are many types of almond flour and you can find some great prices by buying in bulk. If you do buy in bulk, just freeze it so it doesn't go bad before you use it. My go-to grocery store pick-up is Bob's Red Mill (available as a few different flours), because that is the easiest for me to buy locally. Bob's Red Mill has an authentic, coarse grind that will make cookies have more texture. If you want a smoother texture, use a flour that is known for being finely ground. Other flours I use are not exactly like white flour, but they are pretty close. The texture of any of my desserts has never been an issue for me because they all taste so good, and like I said a dozen times before – that is pretty much all I care about it anyway!

Soaking Your Flours

If you want to do the extra step of soaking your almond and coconut flours to reduce phytic acid, that is great. I eat sweets sparingly so I don't always feel the need to do the extra step Start with raw almonds. Soak them in a large bowl and add a pinch of salt. Soak them for 24 hours. Rinse them and fill up the bowl again with water at 12 hours. After they are done soaking, lay them out and add a pinch of salt, then dehydrate them in a dehydrator or in your oven at the lowest temp and the door ajar for another 24 hours. Then roast them at 350 for 10 minutes to really crisp them up. Then you grind up the almonds into a meal/flour. I do this in my food processor, but some people have fancy grain mills. Check out the Nourish & Love webshow episode that explains this process.

Here is a general list of the flours I bake with most often:

Almond Flour

Coconut Flour

Arrowroot Flour

Rice Flour

All-Purpose Gluten-Free Flour

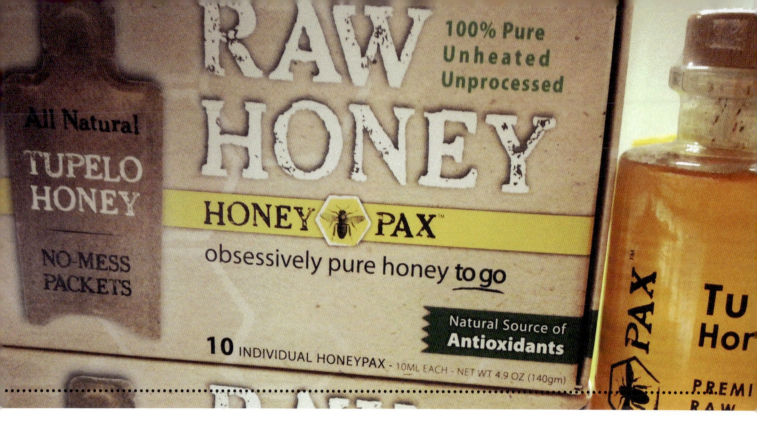

Sugars

Due to the bad rap sugar has gotten, and many people flocking to alternative sweeteners, a variety of industries have made it difficult to discern what you're actually buying.

Raw honey is an amazing sweetener. It has a number of nutrients in it, as well as antibiotic and anitfungal properties. (Not to mention it's great at easing a cough.) Some companies, primarily from China, have decided that it's cool to sell honey flavored corn syrup and still label it as honey. If you're going to use honey as your sugar alternative, please make sure you not only buy raw, but buy local as well. I don't have to tell you about corn syrup!

As far as **cane sugar** goes, you're going to run into more marketing tricks as similar appearing sugars get labeled with all kinds of fancy names. I use rapadura, which is completely unprocessed cane sugar. Rapadura is sold under the brand name Sucanat. Demerara, "Sugar in the Raw" and dehydrated cane juice have all been processed. While they're certainly better than plain white sugar, they're not that much different.

Maple syrup has also fallen prey to greed that's changing the sweetener industry. For a long time we were told to buy Grade B maple syrup because it is far more nutrient dense, but in 2013, that has changed. Everything will now be labeled Grade A with sub-categories for color. Look for the darkest color. It will have the most retained nutrients.

Fruits, starchy vegetables, and a variety of other plant derived sugars, such as date and coconut sugar, can also be used. If you simply cannot use sugar, **real stevia leaf** can be substituted to your taste, although I find that this drastically alters flavor. Be aware of stevia imposters!

Xylitol and other sugar alcohols do not have any kind of proven track record for safety and enough people have come forth complaining of ailments that I just steer clear. **Agave syrup** is another one to just stay away from. It is just as heavily refined and bad for you as corn syrup.

Finally, when buying **vanilla or baking soda** be sure to buy the gluten-free kind.

> **Use the good eggs.**
> When you keep a great stock of real food on hand – like these pasture-raised, farm-fresh eggs – it's easy to cook right!

Build a gluten-free grain-free pantry

Make Old Recipes New

Maybe it's your gramma's pound cake, or the chocolate chip-peanut butter cookies your kids can't get enough of. I bet you've got a traditional recipe you'd love to be able to make grain-free or gluten-free. Start by replacing the bases and starches, and then start working on switching out the liquids and dairy. It's going to take experimentation and practice to get things perfect - but hopefully, even the practice batches are tasty!

I love to organize things in boxes and containers. It's such a pleasure to open up my pantry, and see everything right where it's supposed to be. However you organize your pantry, there's a few things the grain-free, gluten-free baker is going to want to keep on hand. Not all of these things are used in the recipes in this book, but they're things I use often.

Coconut Oil
Maple Syrup
Rapadura/Sucanat Sugar
Coconut or Date Sugar
Raw Honey
Raw Milk
Pastured Eggs
Aluminum-free Baking Soda
Organic, Fair Trade Chocolate Chips
All-purpose Gluten-free Flour

Coconut Flour
Almond Flour
Arrowroot Flour
Rice Flour
Grassfed Butter
Grassfed Lard
Sea Salt
Dehydrated Almonds
Organic Vanilla
Baking Powder

Everyone loves a good cookie!

It's the hardest thing to in the world to say no to. So chocolate chip cookie recipes were the very first thing I started experimenting with. Previously I had been buying Immaculate Baking Co.'s Gluten-free Chocolate Chip Cookies. The kind where you still do the baking, and they taste amazing. So if you are looking for a good store bought alternative, this is your best bet. But then one day it just kind of dawned on me that I bet I could come up with something that tasted just as good. I remember the day I made my first batch of my Gluten-free Chocolate Chip Cookies. I could not wait for my husband to get home from work to give them a try and give me some sort of praise. (I am like a puppy! I constantly need a pat on the pack or someone telling me I did a good job or that I am a good girl.) Anyway, upon him coming in the door, I ran up to him and shoved a cookie in his face and practically screamed, "Try it! It's better than Immaculate Baking Co.!"

I felt like such a BADASS!

Healthy Almond Joy Cookies

3 cups dried coconut

1 cup almond flour/meal

1 cup honey

1/3 cup melted coconut oil

1 tablespoon vanilla

1/2 teaspoon salt

1/2 cup of chopped almonds

1/2 cup of chocolate chips

Whole almonds for tops of cookies

Mix everything together in a food processor, except for the whole almonds (for the top of each cookie.) Use a tablespoon to scoop out and place on cookie sheet. Bake at your lowest temp or in a dehydrator at 115° for about 12 hours, or bake them in the oven at the lowest temp for about 10 minutes, or put them straight in the fridge and eat them cold!

Grain-Free Chocolate Chip Cookies

1½ cups almond flour

1/4 cup butter, softened to room temperature

1/4 cup sugar

1 egg

1/4 teaspoon salt

1/2 teaspoon vanilla extract

1/4 teaspoon baking soda

1 cup chocolate chips

Cream butter and sugar together. Then slowly add in the rest of the ingredients and mix together. Spoon onto a baking sheet and bake at 375° for 12 - 15 minutes.

Gluten-Free Chocolate Chip Cookies

1 cup butter, softened to room temperature

1 cup of sugar

2 eggs

1 teaspoon baking soda

1 teaspoon salt

1 teaspoon vanilla

2½ cups all-purpose gluten-free flour

1½ cup dark chocolate chips

Cream butter and sugar together. Then slowly add in the rest of the ingredients together. Spoon onto a baking sheet and bake at 375° for 12 - 15 minutes.

Great baking starts with great ingredients.

And that means using great flour. I use Bob's Red Mill for Almond Flour, Coconut Flour, White Rice Flour, and their great pizza crusts. You'll find Bob's Red Mill in most major stores like Whole Foods, or you can order their flours online at **bobsredmill.com.** They also have a bunch of other awesome gluten-free and whole-grain products.

Stephanie's Grain-Free Sweet Potato Chocolate Chip

2 cups of cooked sweet potato or pumpkin

2 cups arrowroot

1/2 cup coconut flour

1/2 cup butter, softened to room temperature

1/2 cup coconut oil

1/2 cup shredded coconut

1/2 cup maple syrup

2 cups chocolate chips

2 eggs

1 teaspoon cloves

1 teaspoon nutmeg

1 teaspoon ginger

3 teaspoon cinnamon

2 teaspoon allspice

2 teaspoon baking soda

1 teaspoon salt

Mix ingredients. Bake at 350° for about 20 minutes, or until cookies are firm, but not hard. For a more traditional cookie shape, press down with a fork before baking. This makes at least 2 dozen cookies.

No-Sugar Honey Chocolate Chip Cookies

2 cups almond flour

1/4 teaspoon baking soda

1/4 teaspoon salt

1/3 cup coconut oil or butter softened to room temperature

1/4 cup honey

1 tablespoon vanilla

1 tablespoon milk

1 cup chocolate chips

Mix ingredients and bake at 350° for about 12 minutes.

Pretty vs. Practical

Food media – from television shows, to packaging, to cooking or foodie mags – has been training us for years to think good-looking food is good for you. Anyone who's watched the making of a McDonald's ad knows this ain't exactly true! Because of different, natural ingredients our grain-free cookies, cakes, and other baked goods might not always look they've come out of a magazine. But that's OK. They're much better for us.

These two recipes are some of my holiday favorites!

Simple Sugar Cookie

2 cups almond meal flour

2 tablespoons coconut flour

1/4 cup maple syrup

1/4 cup sugar

1/2 teaspoon unflavored grass fed gelatin

1 teaspoon arrowroot

3/4 teaspoon salt

1/2 cup of butter

1 teaspoon of vanilla

This recipe is a great roll out cut out cookie recipe, so if you want to change the flavor of it, you could swap out the vanilla for ginger and cinnamon for a ginger cookie or add cocoa for a chocolate cookie.

Mix ingredients together till dough forms a ball, refrigerate for one hour. Roll out between two pieces of parchment paper. Bake for 9 - 10 minutes at 350°. You could also roll the dough into a log and freeze. Then slice and bake whenever you want!

Gluten-free Snowman Gingerbread Cookies

2 cups gluten-free flour

(or 1 cup almond flour, 1 cup rice flour)

1 teaspoon baking powder

1/2 teaspoon baking soda

1 teaspoon cinnamon

2 teaspoons ground ginger

1 pinch salt

1 egg

1/2 cup of butter, softened to room temperature

1/4 cup maple syrup

1/2 cup sugar

Cream the butter and sugar. Add the rest of the ingredients slowly and mix together. Then refrigerate for one hour. If you use the all-purpose gluten-free flour you will be able to roll out the dough and do cut out cookies, the grain-free version will be too moist, but you can get creative by rolling the dough into three small balls, increasing in size to make snowmen. Bake at 350° for 15 minutes. Add frosting once cooled.

Go ahead – have a slice!

It's good for your soul – and not that bad for your body! I made my Carrot Cake recipe for dessert for our most recent Christmas Eve dinner, which my entire family had come up for. My younger brothers eat terribly. Lots of soda, chips, fast food, you get the idea. That Christmas Eve dinner was probably the healthiest, most nourishing food they've had their entire lives – but I digress. After dinner I served dessert, but I waited till they gobbled down the cake to tell them it was gluten-free, and that I had made the cream cheese frosting myself with cheese from raw milk. The look of shock on their faces was priceless /The taste was simply delicious.

Walnut-Pineapple Carrot Cake

2 cups grated carrot

1 cup crushed pineapple

2 cups of grain-free/gluten-free flour mix of choice

1 teaspoon cream of tartar

1½ teaspoon baking soda

1/2 teaspoon salt

1 teaspoon cinnamon

3/4 cup sugar

4 eggs

3/4 cup of coconut oil

1/2 cup chopped walnuts (or pecans, almonds, whatever you got on hand!)

Whisk the cream of tartar, baking soda, salt and cinnamon through the flours to make sure it is all evenly distributed. Mix everything else in and mix up the ingredients thoroughly.

This will make you two round cakes, or about 30 cupcakes. Make sure you grease the cake pan well or use liners for the cupcakes. Set the oven at 350° Bake for 20 minutes for cupcakes and 40 minutes for cake. Once the cake has cooled, cover with cream cheese icing (recipe follows later).

M+BL's Walnut-Pineapple Carrot Cake is a guaranteed hit, anywhere!

I-Love-Chocolate Chocolate Cake

Dry Ingredients:

1/2 cup coconut flour

8 tablespoons cocoa powder

3/4 teaspoon baking soda

1/4 teaspoon sea salt

Wet Ingredients:

6 large organic eggs

1/2 cup maple syrup

1/2 cup melted coconut oil

2 teaspoons vanilla

Whisk together the dry ingredients. In a separate bowl blend together the wet ingredients. Pour the wet into the dry and mix together. Spoon the batter into cupcake liners for cupcakes or a cake pan for cake. Set the over a 350°. Bake for 20 - 25 minutes for cupcakes, a little longer for cake. (The clean knife trick works, too!) Cool completely before you frost with icing.

Flourless Chocolate Cake

1 and 1/4 cup cocoa powder

1/2 cup honey

1/2 maple syrup

1 cup coconut oil

3/4 cups butter

6 eggs

1/4 teaspoon cream of tarter

Preheat oven to 325° and grease an 8" pan with coconut oil or butter. Using a double boiler (or just set a heat proof bowl over some simmering water in another pan), combine the following: cocoa powder, maple syrup, coconut oil and butter. Continuously stir on stove until ingredients are melted and smooth. Remove from heat and allow to cool.

In a separate bowl, whip 5 egg whites with 1/4 teaspoon cream of tartar into soft peaks. Don't get any yolk or other oils into the egg whites or they won't whip.

Depending on the thickness of your whites, it can take up to 10 minutes of whipping with an electric beater and whisk. Once you're done with all that whipping, add the 5 reserved egg yolks to the cooled mixture.

Using a rubber spatula, fold in 1/4 of eggs whites to the chocolate, then fold in the rest. Scrape batter into prepared pan. Place pan in a shallow baking dish or roasting pan and pour in enough hot water to reach halfway up side of cake pan (i.e. a water bath.) You'll put this water bath/pan comboe into the oven. Bake at 325° for exactly 30 minutes. The cake will have a thin crust and be gooey in the center. You can also use individual ramekins, like the picture above, instead of a cake pan.

Set cake on a cooling rack to cool completely and then refrigerate until chilled or overnight. To unmold cake, run a knife around the outer edge, then invert on a plate, remove pan and reinvert on another plate. If the cake won't come out of the pan, try placing the bottom in hot water for 30 seconds. You may also leave the cake in the pan, but it can be quite hard to dish out slices without them falling apart.

Cardamom Tea Cake

For the cake:

1/4 cup of butter, softened to room temperature

1 cup of rapadura sugar

2½ cups of gluten-free all-purpose flour

2 teaspoons baking powder

1/2 teaspoon baking soda

2 teaspoons ground cardamom

1/2 teaspoon salt

2/3 cup buttermilk

2/3 cup water

For the crumble topping:

3/4 cup sugar

3/4 cup gluten-free all-purpose flour

1/2 cup of butter

Butter and lightly flour a 13"x9" inch pan. Cream the butter and sugar together. Mix dry ingredients separately and slowly blend into butter-sugar mixture. Mix the buttermilk with the water, pour into dry ingredients and mix all together. Spoon into baking pan.

To prepare topping, mix the sugar and flour together. Cut the butter into small pieces and work into the dry ingredients with your fingers or a pastry cutter, until it is mixed but coarse.

Sprinkle evenly over batter and bake at 350° for 30 to 40 minutes until you can stick a knife in it and it comes out of the cake perfectly clean.

Banana Almond Cupcake Bites

1/2 cup of butter, softened to room temperature

1/2 cup of sugar

3 or 4 ripe bananas

1 teaspoon cinnamon

1/2 teaspoon ground cloves

1 teaspoon baking soda

1/2 teaspoon baking powder

2 cups almond flour

1 cup chopped almonds

1/2 teaspoon vanilla

2 eggs

Cream the butter, sugar and eggs together, then add the bananas, cinnamon and cloves. Then sift the flour, baking soda and powder in a separate bowl, with the nuts, and then slowly blend them together. Or do like me, and just dump it all in one bowl and mix together all in step.

Pour into a bread pan or a cupcake pan and bake at 325° for about a half hour or until you can stick a knife in it and it comes out clean. I always know something is done baking when your house starts really smelling good.

Easy as pie.

There's a reason that phrase exists – pie crust is actually really easy to make, whether you do it old school style with gluten and white flour, or go gluten-free or grain-free. I remember when my mother-in-law taught me how to make her family recipe for pie crust, I thought, "Well, that wasn't so hard at all. What was I so afraid of before?" I needed a lot of hand holding. I would not even dare to make a new recipe unless I had someone in the kitchen with me in case I started panicking and freaking out.

Why? Well for one, it was because I couldn't even properly read recipes from a cookbook way back when – one time I made pesto and I thought one garlic clove meant the whole garlic bulb! I didn't understand the terminology, and since the internet and googling were not the norm back then, I had to physically have someone walk me through a recipe and show me. Seeing how easy it was to make something like pie crust made it easier for me to jump into other recipes.

Gluten-Free Pie Crust with Egg

1/2 cup of butter

1½ cups all-purpose gluten-free flour blend

1/2 cup of sugar

1 whole egg

Cut butter into ½-inch pieces and place it the freezer for 15 minutes. Combine the flour blend, salt and sugar in the bowl of a food processor. Pulse 5 - 6 times to combine. Add the butter and pulse 6 - 8 times or until the mixture resembles coarse meal with some pea size pieces of butter. You can do this by hand, but work quick.

Add ice water 1 tablespoon at a time until the mixture starts clumping together. You want to be careful to not add too much water. If you accidently added more flour, you will just have to eyeball this, and stop right when the dough starts sticking together.

At this point, pat the dough into a ball and put it in the fridge to make sure it is cold before rolling out. You could also store it in the fridge for longer, up to three days, or put it in a freezer bag (smooch it flat and freeze it like a brick to save space) and freeze for later use.

Roll out dough between two waxed pieces of paper. Sprinkling the flour blend on each side so it doesn't stick as well. Transfer to pie dish and gently push into place.

Grain-Free Pie Crust

2 cups almond flour

1 tablespoon coconut flour

1/2 teaspoon sea salt

7 tablespoons butter, softened to room temperature

Mix all ingredients together and form dough into a ball. Press into pie plate. Be sure to use a pie crust cover because almond flour can burn quickly.

Penelope loves helping mama press the pie crust in. You can see the marks from her little fingers!

Throw a pizza party.

Oh, pizza, how I love you. If I ever eat something that is not gluten-free these days, it's pizza from our favorite, local, gourmet pizza place. I swear I actually get a high off all the white flour. I eat that kind of pizza as a rare treat and the rest of the time I make one of these recipes at home. Now, these recipes won't get you high - but they do a pretty good job of satisfying your desire for pizza.

Sweet Potato and Basil Grain-Free Pizza Crust

3 medium sweet potatoes

1 cup almond flour

1 cup water

1 cup egg whites

1/4 cup coconut flour

2 teaspoon basil

1/2 teaspoon baking powder

1/2 teaspoon salt

1 teaspoon garlic powder

Mix ingredients together in a bowl. Then pour batter into a greased skillet and cook it like a pancake. Transfer to cookie sheet or pizza stone and then add all pizza toppings and bake in the oven till heated and melted at 400° for about 5 - 8 minutes.

Twice Baked Grain-Free Pizza Crust

2 cups almond flour

1 cup arrowroot powder

1½ teaspoon baking powder

1 teaspoon salt

2 teaspoons oregano

1/4 teaspoon black pepper

3 eggs

1/2 cup milk

Grease a round pizza stone or cookie sheet. Combine dry ingredients in a large bowl. Whisk to blend together. Add eggs and milk to the dry ingredients. Mix well. It will be runny. Bake crust 8 - 12 minutes at 425°. Remove crust from oven and top with sauce and desired toppings. Bake for another 10 - 15 minutes or until melted.

Gluten-Free Pizza Crust

Honestly, I wish I had some amazing, simple gluten-free crust recipe to give you. Recipes for gluten-free pizza crusts are out there for sure, and taste amazing, but they are complicated as hell. Bob's Gluten-Free Pizza Crust package is really damn good and so easy to mix together.

Spread it on!

Penelope is such a picky eater, that she actually does not like cake or cupcakes, she only wants to eat the icing. If that's the only thing she is going to eat, I'm going to make it right - and these recipes are great.

Honey & Coconut Oil Frosting

1/4 cup coconut oil, softened

1/4 cup raw honey

1 teaspoon vanilla extract

pinch of fine sea salt

Mix the ingredients together. This doesn't make a whole lot but it is really sweet, so you could spread it on thin and be fine.

Chocolate Almond Sprinkles

1 cup almonds

1/2 cup chocolate chips

Put almonds and chocolate into a food processor and grind up till coarse. Sprinkle on cookies while icing is still wet.

Cream Cheese Icing

4 tablespoons butter, softened

4 tablespoons cream cheese

1 teaspoon vanilla

1/2 cup of powdered sugar

Keep doubling this recipe to make a bigger batch of icing. I like to double it one at a time, so I can eyeball it and see how much icing I need.

Beat it until creamy and spread on cupcakes or cake. I like to use homemade cream cheese when I make this icing.

I can't eat homemade cream cheese by itself, I have to sweeten with honey and walnuts and eat it on bread or use it in an icing recipe.

Homemade cream cheese keeps for six months in the fridge sealed in a mason jar or freezer, so I always have some on hand for when I need it for icing on quick notice.

Powdered Sugar & Milk Icing

1 cup powdered sugar

2 tablespoon milk

1/2 teaspoon vanilla

Put all the ingredients in a small bowl and whisk it together. It works in any amount, using the ratios above.

I use this on the sugar cookie recipe. Note that the vanilla makes the frosting, not a perfect white color. This is not a true royal icing either, and it is pretty runny, so you couldn't pipe it through a decorating tip or anything (unless you have mad skills) but it does firm up after applying and looks pretty with sprinkles.

Thanks for reading!

As the Founder and Creative Director of MamaAndBabyLove.com, once a yoga studio and eco-friendly boutique for new parents and now a thriving, real food, natural lifestyle and parenting blog, `thank you for using my cookbook.

I care deeply about nourishing and loving myself so that I can nourish and love my family. It means so much to me to be sharing helpful information with other mothers. I truly hope the recipes in this book help you nourish and love yourself and your own families, as they've nourished me and mine!

You may also be interested in:

M+BL's
Slow Cooker
Freezer Recipes

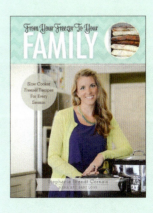

Made in the USA
Lexington, KY
22 September 2014